A Mary Shelley Chronology

Author Chronologies

General Editor: **Norman Page**, Emeritus Professor of Modern English Literature, University of Nottingham

Published titles include:

J. L. Bradley
A RUSKIN CHRONOLOGY

Gordon Campbell
A MILTON CHRONOLOGY

Martin Garrett
A BROWNING CHRONOLOGY
ELIZABETH BARRETT BROWNING AND ROBERT BROWNING
A MARY SHELLEY CHRONOLOGY

A. M. Gibbs
A BERNARD SHAW CHRONOLOGY

J. R. Hammond
A ROBERT LOUIS STEVENSON CHRONOLOGY
AN EDGAR ALLAN POE CHRONOLOGY
AN H. G. WELLS CHRONOLOGY
A GEORGE ORWELL CHRONOLOGY

John McDermott
A HOPKINS CHRONOLOGY

Norman Page
AN EVELYN WAUGH CHRONOLOGY

Peter Preston
A D. H. LAWRENCE CHRONOLOGY

Author Chronologies Series
Series Standing Order ISBN 0-333-71484-9
(*outside North America only*)

You can receive future titles in this series as they are published by placing a standing order. Please contact your bookseller or, in case of difficulty, write to us at the address below with your name and address, the title of the series and the ISBN quoted above.

Customer Services Department, Macmillan Distribution Ltd, Houndmills, Basingstoke, Hampshire RG21 6XS, England

A Mary Shelley Chronology

Martin Garrett

First published 2002 by
PALGRAVE
Houndmills, Basingstoke, Hampshire RG21 6XS and
175 Fifth Avenue, New York, N.Y. 10010
Companies and representatives throughout the world

PALGRAVE is the new global academic imprint of
St. Martin's Press LLC Scholarly and Reference Division and
Palgrave Publishers Ltd (formerly Macmillan Press Ltd).

ISBN 0-333-77050-1

This book is printed on paper suitable for recycling and made from fully managed and sustained forest sources.

A catalogue record for this book is available from the British Library.

Library of Congress Cataloging-in Publication Data
Garrett, Martin
  A Mary Shelley chronology
     p. cm.
  ISBN 0-333-77050-1
  1. Shelley, Mary Wollstonecraft, 1797–1851 – Chronology.
  2. Authors, English – 19th century – Chronology.

PR5398.G37 2001
823′.7–dc21
[B]   2001036492

10   9   8   7   6   5   4   3   2   1
11   10   09   08   07   06   05   04   03   02

Printed and bound in Great Britain by
Antony Rowe Ltd, Chippenham, Wiltshire

Contents

General Editor's Preface

Most biographies are ill adapted to serve as works of reference – not surprisingly so, since the biographer is likely to regard his function as the devising of a continuous and readable narrative, with excursions into interpretation and speculation, rather than a bald recital of facts. There are times, however, when anyone reading for business or pleasure needs to check a point quickly or to obtain a rapid overview of part of an author's life or career; and at such moments turning over the pages of a biography can be a time-consuming and frustrating occupation. The present series of volumes aims at providing a means whereby the chronological facts of an author's life and career, rather than needing to be prised out of the narrative in which they are (if they appear at all) securely embedded, can be seen at a glance. Moreover whereas biographies are often, and quite understandably, vague over matters of fact (since it makes for tediousness to be forever enumerating details of dates and places), a chronology can be precise whenever it is possible to be precise.

Thanks to the survival, sometimes in very large quantities, of letters, diaries, notebooks and other documents, as well as to thoroughly researched biographies and bibliographies, this material now exists in abundance for many major authors. In the case of, for example, Dickens, we can often ascertain what he was doing in each month and week, and almost on each day, of his prodigiously active working life; and the student of, say, *David Copperfield* is likely to find it fascinating as well as useful to know just when Dickens was at work on each part of that novel, what other literary enterprises he was engaged in at the same time, who he was meeting, what places he was visiting, and what were the relevant circumstances of his personal and professional life. Such a chronology is not, of course, a substitute for a biography; but its arrangement, in combination with its index, makes it a much more convenient tool for this kind of purpose; and it may be acceptable as a form of 'alternative' biography, with its own distinctive advantages as well as its obvious limitations.

Since information relating to an author's early years is usually scanty and chronologically imprecise, the opening section of some volumes in this series groups together the years of childhood and adolescence. Thereafter each year, and usually each month, is dealt with separately. Information not readily assignable to a specific month or day is given as a general note under the relevant year or month. The first entry for each month carries an indication of the day of the week, so that when necessary this can be readily calculated for other dates. Each volume also contains a bibliography of the principal sources of information. In the chronology itself, the sources of many of the more specific items, including quotations, are identified, in order that the reader who wishes to do so may consult the original contexts.

NORMAN PAGE

List of Abbreviations

CC	Claire Clairmont
MWG, MWS	Mary Wollstonecraft Godwin, later Mary Wollstonecraft Shelley
PBS	Percy Bysshe Shelley

(Sir) Percy Florence Shelley is often referred to simply as Percy; his father, PBS, was known to his family and early friends by his middle name, Bysshe. (MWS, as far as is known, usually called her husband Shelley.)

Journals	*The Journals of Mary Shelley 1814–1844*, ed. Paula R. Feldman and Diana Scott-Kilvert, 2 vols (continuous page numbers), Oxford, 1987
Letters	*The Letters of Mary Wollstonecraft Shelley*, ed. Betty T. Bennett, 3 vols, Baltimore and London, 1980–8
CC Journals	*The Journals of Claire Clairmont*, ed. Marion Kingston Stocking, Cambridge, Mass., 1968
Clairmont Correspondence	*The Clairmont Correspondence: Letters of Claire Clairmont, Charles Clairmont, and Fanny Imlay Godwin*, ed. Marion Kingston Stocking, 2 vols (continuous page numbers), Baltimore and London, 1995

Collected Tales	*Mary Shelley: Collected Tales and Stories*, ed. Charles E. Robinson, Baltimore and London, 1976
Frankenstein Notebooks	*The 'Frankenstein Notebooks': a Facsimile Edition of Mary Shelley's Manuscript Novel, 1816–17*, ed. Charles E. Robinson, 2 vols, New York and London, 1996
Matthews and Everest	*The Poems of Shelley*, ed. Geoffrey Matthews and Kelvin Everest, vol.1, 1804–1817, London and New York, 1989
Maurice, ed. Tomalin	*Maurice; or The Fisher's Cot*, ed. Claire Tomalin, London, 1998
Novels and Selected Works	Mary Shelley, *Novels and Selected Works*, ed. Nora Crook, 8 vols, London, 1996
On Books and their Writers	Henry Crabb Robinson, *On Books and their Writers*, ed. Edith Morley, 3 vols (continuous page numbers), London, 1938
PBS Letters	*The Letters of Percy Bysshe Shelley*, ed. Frederick L. Jones, 2 vols, Oxford, 1964
Seymour	Miranda Seymour, *Mary Shelley*, London, 2000
Shelley and his Circle	*Shelley and his Circle, 1773-1822*, ed. Kenneth Neill Cameron and Donald H. Reiman, Cambridge, Mass., 8 vols, 1961–86.
Six Weeks' Tour	*History of a Six Weeks' Tour Through a Part of France, Switzerland, Germany, and Holland: with letters descriptive of a sail round the lake of Geneva, and of the Glaciers of Chamouni*, London, 1817
Sunstein	Emily Sunstein, *Mary Shelley: Romance and Reality*, Baltimore, 1989

'Newly Uncovered Letters and Poems'	Betty T. Bennett, 'Newly Uncovered Letters and Poems by Mary Wollstonecraft Shelley', *Keats-Shelley Journal*, vol. 46, 1997, pp. 51–74.
Valperga, ed. Curran	*Valperga: or, the Life and Adventures of Castruccio, Prince of Lucca*, ed. Stuart Curran, Oxford, 1997

Introduction

Why is not life a continued moment where hours and days are not counted ...?

Mary Shelley, letter to Percy Bysshe Shelley, 29 May 1817

Frankenstein and its own 'hideous progeny' of dramatizations (starting with *Presumption* in 1823), public comment and new editions, threatens to take over a chronology of Mary Shelley. Recent work on the manuscripts by Charles E. Robinson in particular has taken us further back towards the (much debated) moment at which she first 'thought of a story' in June 1816. Reviewers often measured her later novels against *Frankenstein*: the more conservative, for instance, shook their heads at the similar excesses of *The Last Man* and welcomed the more domestic element in *Lodore*. For much of her career she usually appears in print as 'the Author of Frankenstein'. This was partly a response to Sir Timothy Shelley's conditions for continuing his meagre financial assistance to her and her son, but also evidently an attempt to capitalize on earlier fame. And even during Mary Shelley's last years, when she has stopped writing and the chronology records mainly details of illness and occasional visits, the odd *Frankenstein* adaptation like the Christmas show *Frankenstein; or the Model Man* at the Adelphi in 1849–50, puts in its incongruous appearance. (The progeny has of course continued to spawn since the author's death in 1851.)

Frankenstein continues central to Shelley and Romantic studies but increasing numbers of readers are becoming aware of her other novels, from *Mathilda* (written in 1819–20) to *Falkner* (published in 1837). A chronological approach helps one to understand something of their gestation period, from the long periods of reading and research which precede the writing of the historical novels *Valperga* and *Perkin Warbeck* to the swifter composition of *Lodore* and *Falkner*, and their publication history. Chronology reminds one forcibly that Mary Shelley's literary activities were considerably more various and, often, complicated, than is suggested by concentration on novels alone. She wrote, among other pieces, more than twenty tales, two mythological dramas, around sixty short biographies of French, Italian, Spanish and Portuguese writers, reviews, essays, poems and, twenty-seven years apart, two rather different travel-books. At the same time she wrote frequently about her travels, reading, other people and herself in her journals and letters. (She felt, justifiably, that her letters lacked the verve of those of her step-sister Claire Clairmont, but they provide, with the journals, a rich source for her personal and literary history from 1814 to 1850.)

Following Shelley as she writes all this reminds one how often her work has a collaborative element. Most obviously, she was involved in preparing many of her husband's manuscripts for the press as well as her own. The involvement was often two-way. For instance while he was in London in October 1817 steering *Frankenstein* through the press, in Marlow she fair-copied two of his Geneva letters, and perhaps 'Mont Blanc', for *History of a Six Weeks' Tour* – itself a joint project. More generally she was influenced by and influenced him, and promoted, edited and helped to shape the reception of his work after his death. She worked also to promote her father's work, as he did hers. She fair-copied, and here and there altered, a number of Byron's major poems.[1] Sometimes less conge-nially, she needed to be willing to adapt to editors' requirements when working for annuals like *The Keepsake*; on more than one occasion she revised a story to make it fit the illustration chosen by the editor.[2]

On a surprising number of occasions Shelley was involved in the production of the work of other writers. She considered, and decided against, the likelihood of getting her old friend John Gisborne's 'Evelina' published in June 1835. She worked on Trelawny's *Adventures of a Younger Son*, counselling expurgation, editing, negotiating with the publishers. She contributed a great deal, over a period of several years, to Thomas Moore's life of Byron: talking to him candidly and at length, writing notes, putting on paper (unfortunately not preserved) what she remembered of the memoirs which had been burned in 1824, and extracting Byron's letters from his correspondents. She edited and completed Clairmont's story 'The Pole' and then arranged its publication with the help of the authoritative fib that it was by 'the Author of "Frankenstein"'. A broader aspect of her collaborative engagement could be said to be her very active career as a reader (detailed quite fully, but with inevitable omissions, in this book) as well as a writer; some interesting work remains to be done on how far her regular reading of other writers' books brought out by her own current publishers affected her writing for them. Shelley also gave such fellow authors as Godwin and Leigh Hunt some very tangible assistance in the form of the money she somehow managed to spare them, and wrote to the Royal Literary Fund to ask for grants for the music critic Edward Holmes and the lexicographer David Booth, husband of her friend Isabella Baxter Booth.

Mary Shelley was involved in collaborative projects not only as a writer but as someone who passionately valued friendship. The ebb and flow of particular friendships and acquaintanceships is another aspect of an author's life which chronology can make unusually evident. She knew that her desire for close and fulfilling relationships was sometimes reciprocated by others only in their hour of need. She was always aware that, good company though he was, Moore would see her much less once she had finished helping him with his work on Byron. But she felt more bitter when Isabel Robinson Douglas, for whom she had done much – even persuading John Howard Payne to arrange a passport for her with the aid of a forged signature in September 1827 (see p. 78) – no longer needed her. More enduringly bitter, although the friendship surprisingly survived, was the discovery that Jane Williams Hogg, Mary Shelley's closest friend in the years after the death of P. B. Shelley and Edward Williams, had been defaming her. Other friends were lost because they died (Lady Paul) or married (Bryan Waller Procter or, more distressingly, Aubrey Beauclerk). She gave up her happy visits to the home of the musician Vincent Novello in response to some whiff of scandal about their relationship in March 1828. Some relationships were more lastingly successful, particularly that with Gee Paul, one of several women in danger of being cast out of society whom she helped and who, in this case, responded so well that she 'shed a charm' over her friend's life (see p. 143). And in her later years her son Percy Florence, while rather disappointingly unambitious, became the 'sheet anchor' of her life; she found her daughter-in-law Jane, Lady Shelley perhaps even more satisfactory. But the unhappy relationships contributed to the depression which is so noticeable a feature of Shelley's Journals, and in which of course other major factors were the deaths of all but one of her children, her widowhood at the age of twenty-four, a powerful sensitivity to the passing of time, and a lifetime of money worries of one sort or another. This is another background against which her works may be read and one reason for their emphasis on friendship – the main way, apart from literary activity, in which she attempted to combat her depression – and, in *Falkner* especially, fidelity. Shelley herself , however, feels that the 'querulous' pages of one of her longest self-analytical journal entries, on 2 December 1834, give 'an imperfect picture' of her since they record her feelings and not her imagination, which 'finds other vents'. Looking in sequence at her remarkably mixed experiences and activities, including those 'vents', should help to give a less imperfect picture.

Notes

1. See, for example, Jane Blumberg, *Mary Shelley's Early Novels*, London, 1993, pp. 71–5, 206–15.
2. See Charles E. Robinson, ed., *Mary Shelley: Collected Tales and Stories*, Baltimore and London, 1976, pp. xvi, 383.

Chronology

1797

August

30   Mary Wollstonecraft Godwin is born at 29 The Polygon, Somers Town, near London, the daughter of Mary Wollstonecraft (1759–97) and William Godwin (1756–1836). Wollstonecraft first met Godwin in 1791. They began a sexual relationship in August 1796 and married on 29 March 1797. She already has another daughter, Fanny (b. 1794, later called Fanny Godwin), the result of her earlier liaison with Gilbert Imlay. Wollstonecraft's *A Vindication of the Rights of Woman* was published in 1792 and *Letters Written During a Short Residence in Sweden, Norway and Denmark* in 1796. Godwin's *An Enquiry Concerning the Nature of Political Justice* appeared in 1793 and *Things as They Are, or the Adventures of Caleb Williams* in 1794. Also in 1794 he argued successfully against the conviction for treason of a group of thirteen fellow reformers, including Thomas Holcroft and John Horne Tooke.

September

10   Wollstonecraft dies of puerperal fever.

1798

January

Publication of Godwin's *Memoirs of the Author of 'The Rights of Woman'* and her posthumous works. The frank accounts of Wollstonecraft's liaison with Imlay, premarital relationship with Godwin, and suicide attempts, provoke much journalistic abuse of both the author and his subject.

A copy of Wollstonecraft's *Lessons* (in her Works) is bound for her sister Everina, perhaps as a first reading book for MWG (Seymour, p. 575 n.14). She grows up with a strong awareness of her mother's memory and frequently reads and thinks by her grave.

1799

Publication of Godwin's *St Leon*.

In winter 1799–summer 1800 Godwin develops what he later calls 'a high degree of affectionate intimacy' (C. Kegan Paul, *William Godwin: his Friends and Contemporaries*, 1876, i.119) with Samuel Taylor Coleridge. According to Lucy Madox Rossetti (*Mrs Shelley*, 1890, p. 28) at some point in MWG's childhood (perhaps before Coleridge's time in Malta in 1804–6), she and CC hide under a sofa to hear the poet recite 'The Ancient Mariner'. They are discovered, but allowed to stay at Coleridge's entreaty. Charles and Mary Lamb are also frequent visitors during MWG's childhood, and the many others who come to the house include Thomas Holcroft, Samuel Rogers, Wordsworth, Maria Edgeworth, Hazlitt, the composer Muzio Clementi, the painters James Northcote and Thomas Lawrence, the writer and scientist Humphry Davy, and the surgeon and chemist Anthony Carlisle.

1801

MWG possibly attends a day school in or near Somers Town (Sunstein 421–2). Much of her education, however, will come from her father.

This autumn Lady Mountcashell, the former Margaret King, whose governess was Wollstonecraft and who will later know the Shelleys and CC in Italy, visits Godwin and probably meets MWG and Fanny.

December

21   Godwin marries his neighbour Mary Jane Clairmont or Vial (1768–1841), whom he has known since early May. She has two children from earlier relationships: Charles (1795–1850) and Jane (1798–1879), who from 1814 will call herself Claire. MWG resents her stepmother from an early stage, whereas until she met PBS, she will later say, her father 'was my God' (*Letters* i.296). The new wife is regarded as difficult, bad-tempered and untruthful by a number of Godwin's friends, especially Charles and

Mary Lamb. But her relationship with her husband is on the whole (with brief tempestuous episodes) happy.

1802

April

4   Mary Jane Godwin gives birth to a son, William, who is either stillborn or soon dies.

1803

Godwin, under the name William Scolfield, publishes his first volume of *Bible Stories* for children.

March

28   Birth of MWG's half-brother William Godwin, Jr.

1805

This summer William and Mary Jane Godwin set up a bookselling and publishing business. Volumes in the Juvenile Library begin to appear. Godwin himself contributes volumes including *Fables, Ancient and Modern* (under the name Edward Baldwin, 1805) and *The Life of Lady Jane Grey, and of Lord Guildford Dudley, Her Husband* (1806, as T. Marcliffe). Mary Lamb's *Mrs Leicester's School* (1809) and Charles Lamb's *The Adventures of Ulysses* (1807) are included in the series, as are volumes by Mrs Godwin, Lady Mountcashell and Eliza Fenwick. MWG, CC and Fanny Godwin read much of the series, some of it before publication.

1806

Godwin, as Edward Baldwin, publishes his *The History of England for the Use of Schools and Young Persons*. This aims, he says in the preface, to use 'a mode of familiar and playful writing' rather than the 'dry and repulsive style' of most such books, which attempt to overload young minds with inessential facts. He is 'accustomed to consult' his children when writing this sort of work. 'I put the two or three first sections of this work into their hands as a specimen.

Their remark was *How easy it is! Why we learn it by heart, almost as fast as we read it!* Their sufferance gave me courage, and I carried on the work to the end.' Whether literally true or not, this perhaps gives some measure of the atmosphere and expectations of the Godwin home. Godwin teaches the children mainly about history, mythology, and literature and encourages them to read widely. The girls are also taught drawing, French and Italian.

1807

August
Mary Jane Godwin and her children and stepchildren move to 41 Skinner Street, London. Godwin joins them in November. The bookshop operates on the ground floor. (The business was formerly conducted in the name of the manager, Thomas Hodgkins, but now in that of Mary Jane Godwin, who is much involved in running it.) The Godwins also rent the printing-shop next door. M. J. Godwin & Co. and the family are often in considerable financial difficulties, necessitating Godwin's unceasing quest for loans.

1808

MWG produces a prose sketch for a continuation of Charles Dibdin's song 'Mounseer Nongtonpaw' by an unknown correspondent of her father. (See *Novels and Selected Works*, 8.397–8.)

August
30   On her eleventh birthday she is taken to Westminster Abbey.

November
Aaron Burr, the disgraced former Vice-President of the United States, visits. He is more impressed on this occasion by William Jr. than by the girls.

1809

MWG probably spends this summer, as do the other children, with the Hopwood family in Somers Town (Seymour, p. 60 n.).

1810

Publication of *The Poetical Class-Book*, edited by Godwin and
W. F. Mylius, including poems by Coleridge, Wordsworth, Byron,
Scott, Rogers, Helen Maria Williams, and Humphry Davy, and
extracts from Milton's *Paradise Lost*. MWG probably reads some of
the material for the first time in this collection.

1811

May

13 (Mon) MWG's hand having erupted with eczema or a similar
condition, she is examined by the surgeon Henry
Cline, who recommends poultices and sea-bathing.
On 17, accordingly, her stepmother takes her to
Ramsgate, where she boards at Miss Caroline
Pettman's school, 92 High Street. Biographers suggest
that the eruption was psychosomatic, inferring dishar-
mony between Godwin and his teenage daughter from
his message to her in a letter to his wife on 18: 'Tell
Mary that, in spite of unfavourable appearances, I
have still faith that she will become a wise and, what
is more, a good and a happy woman' (Paul, ii.184). By
10 **June** she is, Mary Jane Godwin reports, 'decisively
better'. Mrs Godwin and William Jr return to London
later in June.

August

29 (Thurs) Percy Bysshe Shelley (1792–1822) marries Harriet
Westbrook in Edinburgh, having eloped with her on 25.

December

19 (Thurs) MWG returns to London. On 21 Aaron Burr notes that
'Mary has come home, and looks very lovely, but has
not the air of strong health' (*Shelley and his Circle*,
iii.75).

<h1 style="text-align:center">1812</h1>

January

3 (Fri)   PBS initiates correspondence with Godwin, of whose ideas, and those of Wollstonecraft, he is a great admirer.

13   MWG is at the Scot's Corporation Hall to hear Lecture 14 in Coleridge's series on Shakespeare and Milton. He considers Samuel Johnson's *Preface* to Shakespeare, *Othello*, and *King Lear*. She also hears the last three lectures, mainly on Milton, on 16, 20 and 27. Her first sight of George Gordon, Lord Byron (1788–1824) occurs at one of these lectures; he is in the audience on 20 and one other occasion.

22   Burr buys stockings for MWG, CC and Fanny. He goes to see them dressed for the ball they are going to and judges them 'extremely neat, and with taste' (*Shelley and his Circle*, iii.75).

February

15 (Sat) Burr visits the Godwins and hears William, Jr, giving his weekly lecture, inspired by hearing about the lectures of Coleridge and others. The subject is 'The Influence of Government on the Character of the People' and the piece was written by one of his sisters – Burr thinks, no doubt rightly, MWG. 'After the lecture we had tea, and the girls sung and danced an hour' (*Shelley and his Circle*, iii.76). He sees the family again several times in March before he leaves England.

March

MWG's skin eruption has returned, affecting one arm. Cline recommends further sea-bathing, in pursuance of which Godwin arranges for her to stay with an acquaintance, William Baxter, father-in-law of his friend David Booth, at Broughty Ferry, near Dundee.

March

10 (Tues) Publication of Byron's *Childe Harold's Pilgrimage*, Cantos I and II.

June
7 (Sun)
–*c*.14

She sails to Dundee on the packet *Osnaburgh*. On the way she is robbed of money concealed inside her stays (Letters, iii.166). During her two periods with the Baxter family she becomes a close friend of Isabella Baxter, visits Booth several times at Newburgh, goes to St Andrews and Dunkeld, and, she remembers in her 1831 introduction to *Frankenstein*, finds the northern shores of the Tay not 'blank and dreary' but 'the eyry of freedom, and the pleasant region where unheeded I could commune with the creatures of my fancy'. She is already writing, 'but in a most common-place style'; 'It was beneath the trees of the grounds belonging to our house, or on the bleak sides of the woodless mountains near, that my true compositions, the airy flights of my imagination, were born and fostered'.

October
5 (Mon)

PBS meets Godwin and sees him frequently over the next few weeks. Some time this month he also meets CC and Fanny Godwin. PBS, estranged from his father, is in constant financial difficulties but feels it to be his duty – Godwin agrees – to find money for the author of *Political Justice*.

November
10 (Wed)

MWG comes home to London with Isabella Baxter's elder sister, Christy.

11

PBS, Harriet Shelley, and her sister Eliza Westbrook dine with the Godwins. PBS and MWG probably meet for the first time. (Seymour, p. 81, raises the possibility that she stays upstairs to recover from her journey. There has, however, been much talk about PBS in the family since January and it seems likely that she is keen to meet him.) Also at the meal is Dr William Lawrence – the physician consulted about MWG's health before she set off for Scotland, soon to become prominent as a radical scientist. (See 21 March 1816.)

1813

January

23 (Sat)   MWG and Christy Baxter are with Godwin and others at the première of Coleridge's tragedy *Remorse* at Drury Lane.

June

3 (Thurs)   MWG and Christy Baxter sail for Dundee.
23   Birth of PBS's and Harriet's daughter Eliza Ianthe (1813–76).

1814

March

4 (Fri)   PBS arranges to borrow £2593 by selling a post-obit of £8000: agreeing, that is, to repay the £8000 at his father's death. Half the money is intended for Godwin.
20   MWG joins the *Osnaburgh* to sail home. She arrives in London on 30.

April

11 (Mon)   Abdication of Napoleon. (The ensuing peace makes possible the travels of MWG, PBS, and CC later this year.)

May

5 (Thurs)   MWG meets PBS for either the first or second time (see 11 November 1812).
23   Mary Jane Godwin sends Fanny to Wales. Possibly she suspects (probably rightly) that Fanny is falling in love with PBS.

June

By now MWG and PBS are meeting regularly. With CC they often walk from Skinner Street to the greater privacy of an arbour in Charterhouse Square. They also visit Mary Wollstonecraft's grave in St Pancras churchyard. The Godwins have no idea how the relationship is developing.

8 (Tues)   PBS's friend Thomas Jefferson Hogg (1792–1862), visiting Skinner Street with him, has his first glimpse of MWG, later recalled as 'A very young female, fair and fair-haired, pale indeed, and with a piercing look, wearing a frock of tartan'. Hogg asks if she is Godwin's daughter and PBS tells him that she is 'The daughter of Godwin and Mary' (Hogg, *The Life of Percy Bysshe Shelley*, 1858, ii.538).

26   At Mary Wollstonecraft's grave PBS and MWG declare their love. He tells her he no longer loves Harriet and suggests that she has been unfaithful to him. MWG is a strong adherent of her parents' liberal views on marriage. (Her father has by now, however, much modified his opinions.) Either today or on 27 PBS and MWG possibly have sex for the first time. This takes place, according to tradition, in St Pancras churchyard.

July
6 (Wed)   To Godwin's astonishment and horror, PBS reveals his plan to take MWG abroad and asks his consent. Godwin expostulates with him and thinks that he has persuaded him to renounce his 'licentious love'.

8   What Godwin records in his diary as his 'Talk with Mary' seems to persuade her to give up her love.

14   Harriet Shelley comes to London and PBS tells her about his feelings for MWG.

15   Godwin sees Harriet and promises to try to help save her marriage.
           He also continues to see PBS frequently. Unknown to Godwin, MWG continues to receive letters from PBS as well as copies of his *Queen Mab* (1813) and 'A Refutation of Deism' (1814). At some point around now, Mary Jane Godwin subsequently claims, PBS bursts into the house and tries to persuade MWG into a suicide pact. Soon afterwards he takes, but recovers from, an overdose of laudanum.

28   The lovers elope, meeting at about 5 a.m at the corner of Hatton Garden and Holborn. With CC they travel by

post-chaise to Dover and through the night of 28–29 by fishing-boat to Calais, where they stay at Dessein's Hotel.

29   Mary Jane Godwin catches up with the group at Calais. CC agrees to go home with her mother but changes her mind on 30. Defeated, her mother returns to England.

30   The three move on to Boulogne.

August

1 (Mon)   They sleep at Abbeville.

2–8   They stay in Paris at the Hôtel de Vienne. They go to the Tuileries gardens (2). MWG reads some Byron to PBS (3). Increasingly short of money, PBS sells his watch and chain (4). They visit the Louvre and Notre Dame (5). Eventually PBS succeeds in obtaining £60 from a banker or moneylender, Tavernier (7) and, having purchased an ass, the group proceeds to Charenton (8).

9   They sell the infirm ass, buy a mule, and go on to Hôtel Ste-Barbe, Guignes-Rabutin; on 10 they reach Provins and on 11, via the ruins of Nogent-sur-Seine and St Aubin – destroyed by Cossacks during the fighting earlier this year – Ossey-les-Trois-Maisons. 'The distress of the inhabitants, whose houses had been burned, their cattle killed, and all their wealth destroyed, has given a sting to my detestation of war, which none can feel who have not travelled through a country pillaged and wasted by this plague, which, in his pride, man inflicts upon his fellow' (*Six Weeks' Tour*, p. 19). At the time MWG and CC in particular also, less high-mindedly, comment on what they perceive as the dirt of France and the unsociableness of many of its inhabitants.

12   They reach Troyes. On 13 they sell the mule and buy a *voiture* or open carriage. Money is again beginning to run out. They go on to Bar-sur-Aube (14) and Langres (15).

16   They dine at Champlitte-et-le-Prélot and want to take with them a beautiful child, Marguerite Pascal, but her father will not allow it. They spend the night in Gray. On 17 they pass through Besançon and sleep at Morre, where MWG and PBS read part of Wollstonecraft's *Mary, A Fiction*.

18	After a walk in deep forest at Nodz and problems with their *voiturier* they eventually arrive at Pontarlier.
19	The group enters Switzerland and stays at Neuchâtel. Since Paris the journey has cost about £60 (*Six Weeks'*, p. 54). On 20 PBS obtains about £40–50 from a banker. They reach Soleure (21) and Sursee (22). From Lucerne on 23 they go by boat to Brunnen, reading on the way part of Augustin Barruel's *Mémoires pour servir à l'histoire du Jacobinisme*, probably (Journals, pp. 18–19, n.4) in translation.
24	In Brunnen they lodge in an ugly and inconvenient house known as the Château. In the evening, by the lakeshore, PBS reads MWG the account of the siege of Jerusalem in Tacitus' *Histories*, V. On 25 they go on with Barruel and PBS dictates to MWG part of his fragmentary 'The Assassins'.
26	PBS and MWG decide that it is essential to turn back for England since they have only £28 and cannot rely on obtaining more until December, particularly if PBS is not in London (*Six Weeks'*, p. 53). Possibly they do not tell CC how bad the financial situation is. (See Journals, p. 20, n.2.)
27	They cross the lake back to Lucerne. They stay at the Cheval Blanc and read *Richard III* and *King Lear* but are interrupted by CC's 'horrors', probably at the blinding of Gloucester (CC Journals, p. 31).
28–29	They travel, mainly by river, to Basle, sleeping on 28 at Dottingen.
30	They enter Germany. On 31, as they travel along the Rhine, PBS reads to the others Wollstonecraft's *Letters Written During a Short Residence in Sweden, Norway and Denmark*.

September

On the morning of 2 (Fri) they reach Mannheim. Unfavourable wind forces their boat to moor overnight at Gernsheim. MWG and PBS walk for three hours. Conceivably they see Castle Frankenstein in the distance and hear some of the legends associated with Konrad

<table>
<tr><td></td><td>Dippel, who was interested in the reanimation of corpses.</td></tr>
</table>

3	The party reaches Mainz and, on 5, Bonn, where they obtain a *voiture* and drive on to Cologne. On 6–7 they proceed, by an irritatingly slow coach and through uninteresting country (Journals, p. 23), into Holland. On 7 they sleep at Tiel.
8	They arrive at Rotterdam. Their money has now run out, but a captain agrees to accept payment of three guineas each after their passage.
9	They sail for England but bad weather forces a halt at Maarluis until 11. On 10 and 11 MWG works on her (lost) story 'Hate'.
12	A storm and the sickness of MWG and PBS having subsided, they argue with a fellow passenger about the slave trade.
13	They land at Gravesend and continue to London by boat. Eventually PBS succeeds in extracting £20 from his wife Harriet and is able to pay for the passage from Holland. PBS, MWG, and CC stay overnight at the Stratford Hotel, 160 Oxford Street.
14	They read part of Wordsworth's *The Excursion* and are disappointed; 'He is a slave' declares MWG (Journals, p. 25). She reads more of the poem over the next few days and also Southey's *Madoc*. They move into lodgings at 56 Margaret Street, Cavendish Square.
16	Charles Clairmont visits. Mrs Godwin and Fanny come to the window but will not speak to PBS. The Godwins will have nothing to do with the Shelleys; CC can return home only if she too repudiates them.
17	PBS reads Southey's *The Curse of Kehama* to MWG and CC.
18	PBS begins teaching MWG Greek. PBS's friend Thomas Love Peacock (1785–1866) calls, as often during the next few weeks.
19	MWG reads Johnson's *Rasselas*.
20	Between now and 19 October MWG reads her father's *Political Justice*. Her other reading between these dates includes Matthew Lewis's *The Monk*, J. H. Lawrence's *The Empire of the Nairs; or, the Rights of Women*, Edward du

Bois's *St Godwin* and the novel by her father which it parodies, *St Leon*, her mother's *The Wrongs of Woman; or, Maria*, PBS's *Zastrozzi*, and Thomas Jefferson Hogg's *Memoirs of Prince Alexy Haimatoff*. PBS spends much time negotiating financial arrangements, seeing Harriet and sending her now calm, now aggressive letters.

27   MWG, PBS and CC move into lodgings at 5 Church Terrace, St Pancras.

October

1 (Sat)   MWG and CC visit PBS's sisters, Elizabeth and Hellen, at Mrs Hugford's school, Hackney. PBS has been discussing an extraordinary but abortive scheme to 'liberate' his sisters.

7   PBS and CC sit up late and discuss the supernatural. Afterwards CC becomes frightened and he stays with her until, near morning, she begins to go into convulsions and he seeks MWS's help. (See Journals, pp. 32–3 – an entry by PBS – and CC Journals, pp. 48–9). Biographers suggest that such incidents result from the stress of the triangular relationship; certainly they give some indication of the degree of closeness between PBS and CC.

13   MWG, PBS, and CC are at the Theatre Royal, Drury Lane, to see Edmund Kean in *Hamlet*. They sleep at the Stratford Hotel, probably (Journals, p. 35, n. 40) to avoid an expected visit by bailiffs.

19–22   MWG's reading includes *Zadig* (1749) and other works by Voltaire, Alfieri's memoirs, and Godwin's *Caleb Williams*. She also reads his *Essay on Sepulchres* (1809) at her mother's tomb.

PBS's efforts to raise money and avoid creditors and bailiffs continue. Between 23 October and 8 November he lives mostly apart from MWG in order to avoid arrest. She will draw on their life this autumn for the similar experiences of Edward and Ethel Villiers in *Lodore* (1835).

28   Writing to PBS she expresses detestation of her step-mother and claims that 'she plagues my father out of his life' (Letters, i.3).

30	MWG and PBS spend a night at the Cross Keys inn, St John Street.

November

3 (Thurs)	She receives a letter from David Booth announcing that he has forbidden his wife – her friend Isabel Baxter – to write to her.
9	MWG, PBS, and CC move to 2 Nelson Square. PBS's finances have entered a somewhat more settled phase.
13–15	CC temporarily returns to Skinner Street.
13	During the next few months MWG is often unwell, perhaps in connection with her first pregnancy.
30	Birth of Charles (1814–26), son of PBS and Harriet.

In November and December Thomas Jefferson Hogg often visits. MWG has mixed feelings about him, but says that she is beginning to like him more (see e.g. Journals, pp. 49, 51).

December

This month MWG reads several plays by Joanna Baillie.

22	Hogg gives an account of an apparition which she will use in 'On Ghosts' (see March 1824).
28	MWG and PBS go to Professor Garnerin's lecture-demonstration of electricity, gases, and optical illusions at Spring-Gardens Room (Journals, p. 56, n. 1).

1815

In about this year MWG writes 'A History of the Jews', a manuscript essay. (See Jane Blumberg, *Mary Shelley's Early Novels*, 1993, pp. 190–202.)

January

1 (Sun)	Hogg sends MWG a gift and a declaration of love. He is acting with PBS's knowledge; in accordance with PBS's ideals, she is willing, during the next few weeks, to give Hogg some hope that a sexual relationship with her will develop, although it must be delayed until after the birth of her baby. It is unlikely that consummation ever takes place. Some commentators float the possibility that at about this time, again in line with PBS's interest in ideas

of communal living, PBS and CC form a sexual relationship. This is perhaps rather more likely than for Hogg
and MWG, but again – in the absence of evidence – it is
generally felt to be improbable.

c. 10–17   The three move to 41 Hans Place.

29   Between now and early April MWG reads Gibbon's *The
             History of the Decline and Fall of the Roman Empire*.

At some time between this month and March 1816, MWG makes a
transcript of Coleridge's 'France: an Ode' (as 'Ode to France') and
'Fire, Famine and Slaughter', probably from memory or from PBS's
recitation (see *Shelley and his Circle*, vii.9–10).

February

8 (Wed)   The three move again, to 1 Hans Place.

15   MWG and PBS read Byron's *Lara*.

22   MWG gives premature birth to a daughter.

26   Between now and 5 March MWG reads Mme de Staël's
             Corinne; ou l'Italie.

26   Napoleon escapes from Elba.

March

1 (Wed)   Napoleon lands in France.

2   MWG, PBS, and CC move to 13 Arabella Road, Pimlico.

6   The baby dies. MWG sends for Hogg because he is 'so
             calm a creature' (Letters i.11); he stays until the next day
             and then, during his lawyer's vacation, lives at Arabella
             Road from 9 March until 17 April.

18   MWG and Hogg visit Bullock's Museum, Piccadilly. They
             go again with PBS and CC on 20.

22   She goes to the Wild Beasts exhibition at Exeter Change.

23   Out walking with PBS and Hogg, she sees her father and
             Charles Clairmont (who often visits them at this period).
             Godwin avoids speaking to them.

April

21   MWG reads three cantos of Scott's *The Lord of the Isles* and
             looks over Wordsworth's *Poems*, both recently published.

24–27   MWG and PBS stay at the Windmill Inn, Salt Hill, near
             Slough, partly no doubt in order to avoid London credi-
             tors. MWG greatly enjoys being in the country and
             away from CC.

27   MWG, PBS, and CC move to Marchmont Street, Brunswick Square, London.

May

4–13   MWG reads Spenser's *The Faerie Queene*. In April and early May she has also been working hard reading, and 'construing' passages from, Ovid's *Metamorphoses*.

13   CC, after a period of great tension with her stepsister, leaves to live at Lynmouth in Devon.

13   Detailed financial settlement between PBS and his father. PBS's debts are paid and he is given an allowance of £1000 a year. Godwin is given £1000 of the money promised earlier by PBS. Harriet Shelley receives £200 now and per annum.

By the end of the month PBS and MWG have set off for south Devon.

June

MWG and PBS stay at Torquay, later the setting for her 'Maurice, or The Fisher's Cot'.

18 (Sun)   Battle of Waterloo.
            Seymour, p. 156, speculates that they may visit the electrical scientist Andrew Crosse while they are in Devon.

July

1 (Sat)   PBS leaves Torquay to look at a house in Windsor and then returns to London. MWG now or later goes to Clifton, near Bristol. In the absence of an MWG Journal for this period their movements are uncertain; PBS's movements are also uncertain to MWG, who on 27 writes to say that they 'ought not to be absent any longer indeed we ought not' and asks him if CC is with him in London since she has not replied to letters sent to Lynmouth (Letters i.15).

August

4 (Fri)   MWG and PBS move into a furnished house at Bishopsgate, the eastern entrance to Windsor Great Park, later a setting in *The Last Man*.
            Late this month MWG, PBS, Peacock, and Charles Clairmont row up the Thames to Reading, Oxford

(where they visit PBS's former rooms and the Bodleian) and Lechlade, where they probably stay at the New Inn during 4–6 September. The party returns by 10 September. The Shelleys' activities for the rest of the year are again known in less detail than usual because MWG's Journal and letters for the period are lost.

This autumn PBS writes *Alastor; or the Spirit of Solitude.*

This year MWG reads, among many other works, William Beckford's *Vathek*, Rousseau's *Confessions*, Thomson's *The Castle of Indolence*, translations of Bürger's *Lenore* and Goethe's *Werther*, and Germaine de Staël's *De l'Allemagne.*

1816

January
5   CC returns to London.
24   MWG gives birth to William Shelley.

March
This month or early in April CC first writes to Byron.
6 (Wed)   By now MWG and PBS have moved back to London, to 13 Norfolk Street. By 18 they are at 32 Norfolk Street, and on 21 they move to 26 Marchmont Street, London, probably the same lodgings they rented in April 1815.
21   William Lawrence, now professor at the Royal College of Surgeons, gives the first of his inaugural lectures on comparative anatomy. His contributions to the materialist debate are a probable influence on the discussions at Villa Diodati this summer (see 15 June). The Shelleys continue to consult Lawrence on medical matters and it is conceivable that they are present at the lectures.

April
20 (Sat)   CC becomes Byron's lover (*Clairmont Correspondence*, p. 39, n.2).
21   Probable date for MWG's first meeting with Byron (*Clairmont Correspondence*, p. 40, n.1). She visits him

with CC, who does not yet tell her that the relationship is sexual.

23   Byron leaves London and, on 25, England.

May

2 (Thurs)   MWG, PBS, CC, and the baby travel from London to Dover. CC has persuaded MWG and PBS to go to Switzerland so that she can be reunited with Byron and PBS can meet him.

6   The group has arrived at rue Richelieu, Paris. They travel via Troyes, Dijon, Poligny, Champagnolles, and Nion, and arrive (*c.* 13–17) at Hôtel d'Angleterre, Sécheron, Geneva. Here they walk, read, and go boating in the evenings. MWG's months by Lake Geneva were, she tells Thomas Moore on 25 June 1827, 'the happiest of her life' (*Journal of Thomas Moore*, ed. Dowden, 3.1034).

c. 15   MWG transcribes PBS's 'Verses written on receiving a Celandine in a letter from England' (see Matthews and Everest, p. 512).

27   Byron, accompanied by Dr John William Polidori, meets PBS (for the first time), MWG, and CC, on the shore of Lake Geneva.

            PBS and MWG employ Elise Duvillard as nurse for William.

June

1 (Sat)   By now the Shelley group has moved into Maison Chappuis, Montalègre, near Cologny. MWG describes the tremendous thunderstorms which will reappear in *Frankenstein* (*Six Weeks' Tour*, in *Novels and Selected Works*, 8.45; Letters, i.20).

10   Byron and Polidori take up residence nearby at Villa Diodati. There is much daily contact between Maison Chappuis and Villa Diodati, including long conversations into the night. Some time in the next few days, with the weather still unseasonable, the group reads ghost stories from *Fantasmagoriana, ou Recueil d'histoires d'apparitions de spectres ...* translated from German by J. B. B. Eyriès (Paris, 1812). 'These tales', says PBS's preface to the first edition of *Frankenstein*, 'excited in us a

playful desire of imitation'. MWS, in her introduction to the third edition (1831), says that Byron proposes the imitation but that the two 'illustrious poets' and Polidori soon give up. She continues to try to think of a suitable subject. (It is not known whether the ghost-story competition or the conversation about 'the nature and principle of life' – see below – comes first; the latter, as Robinson observes in *Frankenstein Notebooks*, p. lxxvii, may have 'preceded, precipitated, or followed' the former.)

15   Likely date of the conversation which suggests 'the circumstance on which [*Frankenstein*] rests' (PBS's preface). Different descriptions exist. Polidori records on 15 that 'Shelley and I had a conversation about principles, – whether man was to be thought merely an instrument' (*The Diary of Dr John William Polidori*, ed. W. M. Rossetti, 1911, p. 123). The PBS preface refers to 'casual conversation' and MWS in the 1831 introduction recounts more specifically that she was 'a devout but nearly silent listener' to Byron and PBS when they talked about 'the nature of the principle of life, and whether there was any probability of its ever being discovered and communicated'; among other possibilities, 'perhaps the component parts of a creature might be manufactured, brought together, and endued with vital warmth'. (Polidori and CC are also present, probably.) It is while trying to sleep after this conversation that, according to the 1831 account, MWG sees 'with shut eyes, but acute mental vision', 'the pale student of unhallowed arts' kneeling beside 'the hideous fantasm of a man' which is animated by 'the working of some powerful engine' and later 'stands at his bedside, opening his curtains and looking on him with yellow, watery, but speculative eyes'.

16 or 17   Probable date on which MWG begins writing *Frankenstein*. She has now '*thought of a story*' and begins it with 'It was on a dreary night of November', subsequently the opening of volume 1, chapter 3 in the 1818 edition. (These details are written down about fifteen years after the events recalled. MWS may well, however,

be drawing on material in her lost Journal for 14 May 1815 – 20 July 1816.) Between now and August she writes a 'novella-length' ur-text in which Elizabeth is called Myrtella, Clerval is called Carignan, and the Walton frame and story of Safie have yet to be added (*Frankenstein Notebooks*, pp. lx–lxii).

18   Byron recites, according to Polidori's diary, 'some verses of Coleridge's Christabel, of the witch's breast; when silence ensued, and Shelley, shrieking and putting his hands to his head, ran out of the room with a candle … He was looking at Mrs S [i.e. MWG], & suddenly thought of a woman he had heard of who had eyes instead of nipples, which, taking hold of his mind, horrified him'.

22–30   PBS and Byron sail around the lake. MWG continues work on the first version of *Frankenstein*.

July

21 (Sun)   Leaving William at Maison Chappuis with Elise Duvillard, MWG, PBS, and CC set off for Chamonix via Bonneville, Cluses, the Nant d'Arpenas (a striking waterfall), and St Martin-sur-Arve, where they spend the night.

22   They go on to the Cascade de Chède, Servoz, the bridge over the Arve where PBS conceives 'Mont Blanc' (*Poetical Works*, p. 536), and the Glacier des Bossons, and arrive at Hôtel de Londres, Chamonix.

23   They see the Source of the Arvéron. In the evening MWG copies the first part of PBS's letter to Peacock (PBS Letters, i.495–502) on the source and other Alpine sights.

24   They ascend the Glacier of Montanvers in heavy rain. Back at Chamonix MWG reads Mme de Genlis's *Nouveaux contes moraux et nouvelles historiques* and continues with *Frankenstein*.

25   They climb Montanvers again and from the top look down on the Mer de Glace, which MWG will use in *Frankenstein*, volume 2, chapter 2.

26–27   They travel back from Chamonix to the Lake. On 26 MWG asks their guide questions about the local way of life, including patterns of employment. On the evening of 27 they arrive at Villa Diodati and talk with Byron before going back to Maison Chappuis.

28, 30, 31 The group is at Villa Diodati in the evening.

31 Between now and 4 August MWG re-reads Rousseau's *Confessions*.

August

Probably this month, or perhaps in July, MWG transcribes PBS's 'Hymn to Intellectual Beauty'.

2 (Fri) MWG and PBS go to Geneva to buy a telescope for his birthday on 4. In the evening PBS and CC visit Byron; MWG does not go because Byron seems not to want her to, probably because the others are to discuss CC's pregnancy and MWG does not yet know about it (Journals, p. 122 and n.1).

3 MWG, PBS, and CC visit Byron in the evening.

4 While out on the lake with PBS, MWG reads aloud Book Four of Virgil's *Aeneid*. They visit Byron, as on the evenings of 5–7 and 9–11.

12 MWG notes again that she is working on her story (Journals, p. 124). 'Write', she notes on 16 and 17 and several times later this month.

13 The three again go to Villa Diodati in the evening, MWG for the last time. Feldman and Scott-Kilvert suggest that she stops going there in order to minimize gossip (Journals, p. 125, n.1).

17 The baby is unwell. Dr Polidori comes down to Maison Chappuis.

18, 20, 21 Byron visits Maison Chappuis. On the evening of 18 he, PBS, and Matthew 'Monk' Lewis discuss ghosts. (MWG does not meet Lewis.)

21 The Shelleys talk about *Frankenstein*, 'most likely ... about ways to transform her "story" into a "book"' (*Frankenstein Notebooks*, p, lxxxi); 'Shelley urged me to develope the idea at greater length' (1831 introduction). Between about now and April 1817 she expands the novella into a draft two-volume novel.

22 MWG and PBS go to Geneva to see the cemetery. She finds it ugly.

24 and 25 Byron visits.

26 PBS reads Coleridge's 'Christabel' to MWG before they go to bed. She reads it again the following day.

28	Polidori and Byron visit.
29	MWG, PBS, CC, the baby and Elise set off for England. They sleep at Morez today and go on via Dôle and Rouvray (30) .

September

1 (Sun)	They dine at Auxerre and stay the night at Villeneuve-la-Guyard. On 2 they visit the forest and palace of Fontainebleau and reach Versailles, where they see the palace of Versailles on 3 before going on probably to Vernon or Gaillon (Journals, p. 134, n.1). On 4 they visit Rouen, see the cathedral, and sleep at Yvetot, and on 6 arrive at Le Havre.
7–8	They sail to Portsmouth.
9	PBS goes to London to deliver Byron manuscripts to John Murray and deal with financial affairs. MWG, CC, William, and Elise Duvillard, travel via Salisbury (9) to Bath (10), where CC's baby is to be born away from the Godwins and London publicity. On 11 they find lodgings at 5 Abbey Churchyard. About a week later CC moves to 12 New Bond Street, Bath.
11–14	MWG reads Scott's *The Antiquary*.
16 and 18	She probably resumes work, temporarily, on her novel (see *Frankenstein Notebooks*, p. lxxxi.)
19	She travels to Maidenhead. With PBS and Peacock, who meet her there, she walks to Marlow.
19–20	She reads Rousseau's *Emile*.
20	They visit Medmenham Abbey, near Marlow.
20–23	MWG's reading includes Richardson's *Clarissa*, whose epistolary form may be an influence on *Frankenstein*.
25	MWG, with PBS, returns to 5 Abbey Churchyard, Bath. MWG takes regular drawing lessons over the next few months.

October

2 (Wed) – 3	MWG reads Lady Caroline Lamb's *Glenarvon*.
9	Fanny Godwin commits suicide in Swansea.
18–28	A period of sustained work on *Frankenstein*.
28–31	In connection with work on her novel, MWG reads Sir Humphry Davy's *Elements of Chemical Philosophy* (1812),

George Anson's *A Voyage Round the World* and E. Ysbrants Ides's *Three Years Travels from Moscow*. Probably by 27 she has drafted Walton's letters and what will become volume 1, chapters 1 and 3. Chapter 2 is probably inserted by 28 (*Frankenstein Notebooks*, pp. lxxxii–iii).

November

During the first few days of the month she continues to read Davy. Work on the draft *Frankenstein* continues between now and mid-December.

16   MWG reads 'old voyages' (*Journals*, p. 146).

20   She finishes writing the Justine story.

17–21 or 22 PBS reads Milton's *Paradise Lost* – one of Frankenstein's creature's texts – aloud. Recently, also like the creature, he has been reading Plutarch's *Lives*.

18   Byron's *Childe Harold*, Canto Three, is published.

December

4 (Wed) PBS goes to Marlow to look for a house.

5   MWG tells him that she has finished a very long fourth chapter of *Frankenstein*. This is probably the equivalent of the much shorter volume 2, chapter 4, in the published text of 1818, covering Safie's arrival and her language learning. At this stage she is called Maimouna, and later briefly Amina (*Frankenstein Notebooks*, pp. lxxxiii, lix–lx).

6–9   She may continue to write about Safie/Maimouna while reading Wollstonecraft's *Vindication*.

9 or 10 Suicide, by drowning, of Harriet Shelley.

14   PBS comes back to Bath.

17   PBS is in London, trying to obtain custody of his children by Harriet. MWG writes to say that she looks forward to welcoming them into the family.

24   Godwin writes to his daughter to encourage her to marry PBS. She comes to London probably on 27 or 28. Godwin visits her on 28, probably at the house of Leigh and Marianne Hunt.

29   MWG and PBS are at Skinner Street; the Godwins can be reconciled with the about-to-be-married couple.

30	Marriage of MWG (from now on MWS) and PBS at St Mildred's Church, Bread Street, London. The Godwins are present. Later both MWS and her daughter-in-law Jane, Lady Shelley, work to give the impression that the marriage took place earlier in the Shelleys' relationship.

1817

January
1 (Wed)	The Shelleys return to Bath. Work on the draft *Frankenstein* continues until at least 10.
6	PBS goes back to London in pursuit of his claim for custody of his children by Harriet.
12	Birth of CC's daughter by Byron, at first called Alba, later Allegra.
24	The custody case is adjourned.
24	Between now and 15 February MWS reads Sidney's *The Countesse of Pembrokes Arcadia*.
26	MWS goes to London, leaving William in Bath.
29	She sees George Colman the Elder's *The Jealous Wife* and Isaac Pocock's *The Ravens; or, the Force of Conscience* at Covent Garden.
30	She stays overnight with Leigh and Marianne Hunt at their house in the Vale of Health, Hampstead.

February
1 (Sat)	MWS and Marianne Hunt go to Mozart's *The Marriage of Figaro* at the King's Theatre. She continues to see much of the Hunts throughout this month and early March.
5	MWS meets John Keats and John Hamilton Reynolds at dinner at the Hunts'.
7	The Shelleys take up residence with the Hunts.
8	They dine at Horace Smith's.
9	After music and supper at the Hunts' a discussion with Hazlitt on monarchy and republicanism goes on until 3 in the morning.
10	MWS talks to Charles and Mary Lamb at the Godwins'.
11	She sees Kean as Shylock in *The Merchant of Venice* at Drury Lane.

12	John Keats and his brother George take tea and supper at the Hunts'; Keats visits again on 15.
16	MWS and PBS see Hazlitt and his wife, Godwin, and his friend Basil Montagu.
18	CC, Allegra, William, and Elise come to London from Bath. CC and Allegra live separately in lodgings.
20–21	MWS reads Hazlitt's and Hunt's *The Round Table*.
22	She goes to *The Beggar's Opera* and other pieces at Covent Garden with the Hunts and Elise.

March

2 (Sun)	The Shelleys move to Marlow. They stay with Peacock and his mother until the house they are renting is ready, and continue to see Peacock often during their time in Marlow.
11–13	MWS is in London. She sees Kean in Maturin's *Manuel* at Drury Lane.
18	The Shelleys move into Albion House, West Street, Marlow. Another period of intensive work on *Frankenstein* begins.
18	MWS expresses dislike of Hogg, who is staying with Peacock (Letters, i.35).
27	The Lord Chancellor, Lord Eldon, refuses PBS custody of his children by Harriet.
c. 31	CC joins the Shelleys in Marlow, leaving Allegra temporarily behind in order to conceal her existence from the Godwins and others.

April

2 (Wed) – 6	Godwin visits.
6	The Hunts arrive, bringing Allegra with them. They live with the Shelleys until 25 June.
10	MWS starts correcting *Frankenstein*. (For further details see *Frankenstein Notebooks*, p. lxxxv.)
18	Between now and 13 May she fair-copies the novel. The fair copy will be used also as a printer's copy (*Frankenstein Notebooks*, p. lxxxv).

May

This month she transcribes PBS' 'Marianne's Dream'.

| *c.* 10 (Sat) – 13 | PBS 'for unknown reasons' writes out the last 12¾ pages of the *Frankenstein* fair copy. MWS in turn copies his version. (See *Frankenstein Notebooks*, p. lxxxv.) |

14	She writes a preface for *Frankenstein* (Journals, p.169), but in the event a preface by PBS, written in September this year, will be printed.
22	The Shelleys go to Kingston-on-Thames and then, on 23, to London, where they see Mozart's *Don Giovanni* at the King's Theatre. On 24 they visit the Royal Academy Exhibition.
25	They see Hogg and Hazlitt.
26	The publisher John Murray apparently likes *Frankenstein* (Journals, p. 171). But by 29, apparently on the advice of William Gifford, Murray has decided not to buy the copyright; see also 18 June.
26	PBS returns to Marlow.
27	MWS sees Kean in John Brown's *Barbarossa* at Drury Lane.
28	She reads the third canto of *Childe Harold*, and remembers PBS first reading it to her the previous summer at Maison Chappuis. The poem, and this thought, give her a melancholy awareness of the passage of time (Journals, pp. 171–2; Letters, i.36).
30	She walks to the unfinished new Waterloo Bridge with her father and sups with the Lambs.
31	She returns to Marlow.

June

4 (Wed)	Between now and January 1818 she works carefully through Tacitus' *Annales*.
17	She spends the day at Medmenham Abbey.
18	*Frankenstein* is refused by Murray. MWS sends the manuscript to Godwin and he sends it to another (unknown) publisher, again unsuccessfully.

July

13 (Sun)	She is copying PBS's translation of Aeschylus' *Prometheus Bound*.
26–31	Hogg visits Marlow.
31	She receives a 'disagreeable' letter from Isabel Booth (see 3 November 1814).

August

3 (Sun)	PBS sends the manuscript of *Frankenstein* to the publisher Charles Ollier, who at some point in the next fortnight or so – perhaps as early as 6 – refuses it.

Between 9 and 13 and perhaps until later in the month, MWS fair-
      copies the first section of *Six Weeks' Tour*, based on the
      Journals of summer 1814.
10–29   Her reading includes a number of plays by Beaumont
      and Fletcher.
22   The Lackington publishing company, one of whose
      special fields is ghosts and the occult (*Frankenstein
      Notebooks*, p. lxxxvii), is showing interest in *Frankenstein*.
30   MWS's twentieth birthday.

September
1 (Mon) – 4 William Baxter, father of MWS's friend Isabel, comes to
      Marlow. He is surprised and impressed by PBS, and
      writes to tell Isabel so on 3 (*Journals*, p. 179, n.3).
2   Birth of the Shelleys' daughter Clara Everina. Some time
      between now and 19 Lackington agrees terms for the
      publication of the novel; the author will receive a third
      of receipts after publishing expenses have been
      deducted (*Novels and Selected Works*, 1. xciv). The
      amount due will be, in the event, £41 13s. 10d.
      (*Frankenstein Notebooks*, p. xcii).
19–25   The Hunts visit.
23   PBS and CC go to London. CC returns to Marlow on 27,
      but PBS remains in London much of the time between
      now and late November engaged in various legal,
      financial, and publishing affairs. Proofs of *Frankenstein*
      are printed between now and 3 November; revised
      proofs between now and 20 November.
25–29   William Baxter stays again. By December, however, he
      has decided, probably under the influence of his son-in-
      law Booth, to end his intimacy with the Shelleys.

In late September and early October the Shelleys debate whether
they should move to Italy.

October
6 (Mon)   PBS has offered a book by CC to Lackington and to
      Taylor & Hessey. Both have rejected it.
12–14 or 15 MWS is copying and adapting PBS's letters from Geneva
      for the second part of *Six Weeks' Tour*. She may also copy

	his 'Mont Blanc' from draft for its inclusion in the volume (Matthews and Everest, p. 534).
13	With her father, who stays between 12 and 15, she visits John Hampden's monument at Great Hampden (used in *Frankenstein*, volume 3, chapter 2). By 13 he has read the proofs of the first volume of her novel; proofs arrive in time for him to finish the third volume on 24 November.
28	PBS sends 'considerable alterations' to *Frankenstein* to Lackington (PBS Letters, i.419). It is now generally accepted that most of these alterations are by MWS, although there were clearly also contributions by PBS. For the most authoritative account of the nature of PBS's collaboration in the work more generally, correcting some frequent misconceptions, see *Frankenstein Notebooks*, pp. lxvi–lxxi.

November

In the first two weeks of this month MWS translates 'Cupid and Psyche' from Apuleius' *The Golden Ass*.

6 (Thurs)	Publication by T. Hookham and C. and J. Ollier of MWS's (anonymous) *History of a Six Weeks' Tour Through a Part of France, Switzerland, Germany, and Holland: with letters descriptive of a sail round the Lake of Geneva, and of the Glaciers of Chamouni* (Letters III and IV by PBS). The book costs either 4s. 6d. or 5s. (*Novels and Selected Works*, 8.6, n.8). *Blackwood's Edinburgh Magazine* III (April–September 1818), pp. 412–16, praises the book's attractive simplicity at the implied expense of Lady Morgan's more ambitious and outspoken *France* (1817). The review is possibly by Walter Scott (*Novels and Selected Works*, 8.3–4, 7 n.17). *The Eclectic Review*, 2nd series, vol. 9, May 1818, wonders whether the whole account is invented.
8	She joins PBS in London at 19 Mabledon Place, Euston Road. They see the Hunts and Godwin often, Baxter on 9 and, with his son-in-law Booth, on 13, the publisher Charles Ollier on 11, Keats on 18.
10	MWS is reading Dante, probably in Henry Cary's translation. On 12 she reads Coleridge's *Zapolya*.

| 19 | MWS returns to Marlow. PBS follows several days later. |
| 29–30 | PBS reads aloud his *Laon and Cythna*. |

December

1 (Mon) – 2	MWS reads Godwin's newly published *Mandeville*.
3	MWS's dedication of *Frankenstein* to Godwin is sent to the publishers.
4–10	She copies Peacock's poem *Rhododaphne; or, the Thessalian Spell*.
15	She is probably involved in discussions of alterations to PBS's *Laon and Cythna* designed mainly to reduce the danger of prosecution for blasphemous libel (Journals, p. 187, n.1).
26–28	Horace Smith stays.

500 copies of *Frankenstein* are printed. Advance copies arrive on 31.

1818

January

Close contact with Peacock continues.

| 1 (Thurs) | Publication of *Frankenstein: Or, the Modern Prometheus* (3 volumes, Lackington, Hughes, Harding, Mavor and Jones). A number of the reviews assume that the author is PBS. Verdicts range from John Wilson Croker's 'tissue of horrible and disgusting absurdity' in the *Quarterly Review* for January to Walter Scott's more searching account in *Blackwood's Edinburgh Magazine* for March. Scott praises 'the author's uncommon powers of poetic imagination'; 'It is no slight merit … that the tale, though wild in incident, is written in plain and forcible English, without exhibiting that mixture of hyperbolical Germanisms in which tales of wonder are usually told' and the ideas 'are always clearly as well as forcibly expressed'. Probably at some point in January–March PBS also writes, but does not publish, a review in which he states the moral of the novel as 'Treat a person ill, and he will become wicked. Requite affection with scorn; – let one being be selected, for whatever cause, as the |

refuse of his kind – divide him, a social being, from society, and you impose upon him the irresistible obligations – malevolence and selfishness'. For publication of this piece see under October 1831.

3–19   Hogg visits.

12   CC writes to Byron praising *Frankenstein* as a work of genius which no one would imagine 'so young a person' could have written. Whatever her personal envy, she delights in the fact that MWS 'is a woman and will prove in time an ornament to us and an argument in our favour' (*Clairmont Correspondence*, p. 111).

14–16   MWS reads Scott's *Guy Mannering*.

20–22   Godwin and William Godwin Jr visit.

29   PBS, CC and Peacock go to London.

29   MWS re-reads the second canto of *Childe Harold*. Between 29 and 31 she reads Laurence Sterne's *Tristram Shandy* and *A Sentimental Journey*.

February

5 (Thurs)   PBS and CC return to Marlow from London. PBS goes back to London on 7, and the others follow on 9, staying that night in a hotel in Great Russell Street.

8   MWS reads Byron's *The Giaour* and *The Corsair*. She reads his *Lara* on 9.

10   The Shelley group moves into 119 Great Russell Street. MWS, PBS, and CC go to Mozart's *Don Giovanni* at the Haymarket; they see it again on 21 and on 7 March.

11   They see the Hunts, as often during the next month, when on various occasions they are also in company with Peacock, Hogg, and Horace Smith. They see less of the Godwins, mostly because of Godwin's anger at receiving only a small portion of the money raised by PBS's latest post-obit loan, taken out on 30 January.

13   MWS examines the Parthenon frieze ('Elgin Marbles') at the British Museum, which she visits again on 17.

16   She is at Henry Hart Milman's *Fazio* and the pantomime *Harlequin Gulliver* at Covent Garden.

19   She copies PBS's incomplete *Rosalind and Helen* (finished this August).

23   At Drury Lane she sees Edmund Kean in a musical drama
            based on Byron's *The Bride of Abydos*, and on 24 *The
            Marriage of Figaro* at the King's Theatre.

March
3 (Tues)   Isabel Baxter Booth has come to London but does not,
            apparently, see MWS.
5   MWS sees Isaac Pocock's *The Libertine*, based on *Don
            Giovanni*, at Covent Garden.
8   The Shelleys meet the famous musician Vincent Novello
            at the Hunts'.
9   William, Clara, and Allegra are christened at St Giles-in-
            the-Fields. Baptism of the first two aims 'to secure their
            legitimate status at a time when their parents were full of
            fears about the Lord Chancellor's seemingly malevolent
            attitude to Shelley's children' (Seymour, p. 198). This
            fear and the desire to avoid Godwin with his belief that
            PBS is depriving him of promised or available money are
            among the reasons for the group's imminent departure
            for Italy. They also want to see Byron and sort out
            Allegra's future with him.
10   The Shelleys, the Hunts and Peacock see Rossini's *The
            Barber of Seville* at the King's Theatre. Godwin visits.
11   MWS, PBS, CC, the children, Elise, and another servant,
            Milly Shields, set off for Italy. After a night at the York
            Hotel, Dover, they sail to Calais on 12 and then proceed
            to St Omer (13), Douai (14), La Fère (15), Reims (16), St
            Dizier (17), Langres (18), Dijon (19), Tournus (20), and
            Lyon, where they spend 21–25 at the Hôtel de l'Europe,
            visit the Ile de Barbe, and attend a comedy, *L'Homme gris
            et le physiognomiste*.
25   They go on to Tour du Pin, Chambéry (26–27), St Jean le
            Maurienne (28), and Lanslebourg (29); they cross Mont
            Cenis on 30 and reach Turin on 31.

April
1 (Wed)   They go to the opera in Turin before continuing, on
            2–4, to Milan, where they stay at the Locanda Reale
            until 9, visit the cathedral (5), and go twice (5 and 7) to
            La Scala, where they particularly enjoy Salvatore
            Viganò's ballet *Otello*.

9–12	MWS and PBS look for a house in Como and elsewhere on Lake Como, but give up and return to Milan. They go to the cathedral and La Scala again. MWS's reading includes Italian translations of Samuel Richardson's *Pamela* and *Clarissa*. (She first read these novels in 1816 and 1815 respectively.) She also works at 'Italian exercises'.
28	Elise takes Allegra to Byron in Venice. In London the fourth canto of his *Childe Harold's Pilgrimage* is published.

May

1 (Fri)	The group leaves Milan, sleeping that night at Piacenza and then at Parma (2) and Modena (3). They dine at Bologna and sleep at a mountain inn (4), Barbarino (5), and the inn or hamlet of La Scala (6).
6–9	They stay at the Tre Donzelle, Pisa.
9	They arrive at Livorno, staying at first at the Aquila Nera and then at the Croce di Malta. Maria Gisborne, once a friend of MWS's parents, calls with her husband, John. On 10 MWS has a long talk with Mrs Gisborne about Godwin and Wollstonecraft. The Shelleys see one or both Gisbornes almost every day, and often also Maria Gisborne's son Henry Reveley.
23–25	MWS transcribes the manuscript *Relazione della morte della famiglia Cenci … 1599*. She will translate it at some point between now and the summer of 1819, and it will be published in the second edition of PBS's *Poetical Works* in 1839. According to MWS's note there, he originally wanted her to write what became *The Cenci*.
26–28	PBS goes to Bagni di Lucca to find accommodation.
26	Between now and 19 July MWS reads Ariosto's *Orlando Furioso*.
28	The Shelleys inspect Henry Reveley's steam engine, intended eventually to power a Mediterranean steamer.

June

8 (Mon)	Godwin has written 'the plan of a book … to be called "The Lives of the Common-wealth's Men"'. He will never write it, but feels that MWS might; 'I should think

she is perfectly capable'. On 25 July PBS agrees that this is 'precisely the subject for Mary' but indicates that she would be unlikely to undertake it because of difficulties in obtaining relevant books while in Italy (PBS *Letters*, ii.21 and n.2).

11   The Shelley party moves to Casa Bertini, Bagni di Lucca. Here Paolo Foggi enters their employment.

Between 12 and 25 MWS' reading includes Gibbon's *Decline and Fall*.

14   In response to Scott's favourable review of *Frankenstein* in March, MWS writes to thank him and to explain that she is the author and not, as he inferred, PBS.

30   MWS and PBS ride to the Prato Fiorito, above Bagni di Lucca.

July

5 (Sun)   The Shelleys and CC watch dancing at the Casino, as on 12 and on 2 and 9 August.

20   Between now and 6 August MWS transcribes PBS's translation of Plato's *Symposium*. She reads his *The Revolt of Islam* (the revised *Laon and Cythna*) at the end of this month and the beginning of the next.

25–28   She reads Tasso's *Aminta*.

27   The Shelleys and CC are at a 'Festa di Ballo' in the evening.

August

In the first weeks of the month the Shelleys and CC often walk or ride in the evenings (but CC stops riding after a fall on 8).

1 (Sat) – 27 MWS reads Tasso's *Gerusalemme liberata*.

17   PBS and CC set off for Venice. CC is worried about Allegra, whom Byron has sent to live with Richard Belgrave Hoppner, the British consul in Venice, and his wife Isabella.

21   MWS notes in her journal that her daughter Clara is unwell.

23–24   PBS is with Byron at Palazzo Mocenigo in Venice. Since CC would be most unwelcome, PBS claims that she – and MWS and the children – are in Padua. Byron offers PBS and the others the use of Villa I Capuccini in Este and says that Allegra can join them there for a time. In order to conceal his lie about the whereabouts of the women and children, he writes to tell MWS to proceed to Este as swiftly as possible.

25   The Gisbornes come to stay with MWS.

28   PBS's letter (see 23–24) arrives.

30   Peacock, writing to PBS, says that at Egham racecourse people kept asking him about *Frankenstein* and concludes that it is becoming universally familiar.

31   MWS and her children set off for Este. Maria Gisborne accompanies her as far as Lucca. For the rest of the journey she is accompanied by the servants Paolo Foggi and Milly Shields. They reach Florence in the evening.

September

2 (Tues)   After a day in Florence – made necessary while they wait for an official signature on their passport – MWS and her party continue their hot, rushed journey, arriving at Este on 5. By then Clara, whose first birthday was on 2, is violently ill with dysentery.

In Este, by 14, MWS has begun to translate Alfieri's *Myrrha*. She reads most of Alfieri's other plays over the next few days.

16   PBS and CC, who are both unwell, go to Padua for the day to seek medical attention.

22   PBS and CC go to Padua again. He goes on to Venice while she returns to Este. PBS writes to tell them to meet him in Padua on 24.

24   It becomes apparent that Clara is desperately ill. The journey to Padua has made her condition worse. The Shelleys take her to Venice to see Dr Aglietti, but she dies in her mother's arms very soon after reaching the city. CC goes back to Este to be with Allegra and William.

Between 24 and 29 MWS and PBS stay with the Hoppners.

26   She sees Byron on the Lido, where he often rides and where, in the old Protestant cemetery, Clara is buried.

27   MWS reads Byron's *Childe Harold*, Canto Four, and then visits the Doges' Palace, the Accademia gallery (with the Hoppners), and Byron at Palazzo Mocenigo. There she also sees Byron's mistress Margarita Cogni.

28   Byron calls on the Shelleys.

29   They return to Este.

30	MWS starts transcribing the manuscript of Byron's *Manfred*. She finishes on 2 October.

October

2 (Fri) – 3	She transcribes Byron's manuscript *Ode on Venice*. On 3 she expresses interest in reading or copying the first canto of *Don Juan*. Possibly about now she also reads his subsequently destroyed memoirs. 'There was not much in them' (Letters, i.437).
11	MWS, PBS, William, and Elise go to Padua and (12) Venice, where the unwell William can be seen by a good doctor. In Venice they stay at the Hôtel Grande Bretagne and dine regularly at the Hoppners'. PBS, usually without MWS, is much in company with Byron.

Between 14 and 20 her reading includes Byron's *Beppo* and she sees Rossini's *Otello* with the Hoppners.

20	At the Hoppners', Cavaliere Angelo Mengaldo tells three ghost stories. MWS writes them down; she will use the second in 'On Ghosts' (see March 1824).
24	PBS goes to Este to collect Allegra. His attempts to persuade Byron to leave her with CC have failed.
29	PBS arrives with Allegra. Byron probably sends her again to the Hoppners.
31	The Shelley group travels to Padua.

November

1 (Sun)	They reach Este.
5	PBS, MWS, CC, William, Elise Duvillard, Paolo Foggi, and Milly Shields set off for Naples. They reach Rovigo on 5 and spend 6–8 in Ferrara, where they see the Ariosto and Tasso sites and memorabilia. During 8–11 they are at Bologna, where on 9 and 10 PBS and MWS admire paintings including work by Correggio and Guido Reni at the Accademia.
	They travel on to Faenza (11), Cesena (12), Rimini and Cattolica (13), Pesaro, Fano, and Fossombrone (14), Scheggia (15), Foligno (16), Spoleto and the Temple of Clitumnus (17), Terni and its waterfall (18), Nepi (19), and across the Campagna to Rome (20).

During their week in Rome the group engage in active sightseeing: they go to St Peter's on 21, the Colosseum first on 22 and several more times over the next few days (MWS takes William there and sketches on 25), Santa Maria Maggiore and Santa Maria degli Angeli (23), San Paolo fuori le Mura and the Via Appia Antica (26), and much else.

27   PBS goes ahead to look for accommodation in Naples. MWS and the others follow via the Campagna and Velletri (28), the Pontine Marshes and Terracina (29), and Gaeta and the so-called villa and tomb of Cicero, the setting and associations of which particularly impress MWS (30).

December

1   MWS, CC, William, and servants rejoin PBS at 250 Riviera di Chiaia, Naples. This will be the Shelleys' and CC's home until the end of February 1819.

5   Visit to Herculaneum.

8   The group goes by boat to the Bay of Baiae (Baia) and visits the nearby Lago d'Averno, Elysian Fields, and Solfatara.

During 12–14 MWS re-reads Madame de Staël's *Corinne*. Other reading at this time – as at intervals between June this year and July 1820 – includes Livy's history of Rome.

13   The group goes to Rossini's *Ricciardo e Zoraide* at the Teatro San Carlo.

15   They visit the alleged Tomb of Virgil (as again on 28) and the Grotto of Posillipo.

16   They go up Vesuvius.

18–19   MWS copies PBS's 'Lines Written Among the Euganean Hills'. Earlier in the year she persuaded him to complete this poem and *Rosalind and Helen*.

19   They see 'most beautiful statues' (Journals, p. 245) at the Studii.

20   MWS corrects *Frankenstein*, presumably for a proposed second edition.

22   They are delighted by Pompeii.

Between 23 of this month and 9 January 1819 she reads Virgil's *Georgics*. She tells Maria Gisborne that it is in many ways the most beautiful poem she has read; her pleasure is enhanced by reading in the area where Virgil wrote (Letters, i.85).

24 December – 3 January 1819 PBS reads aloud a French translation of Winckelmann's history of ancient art.

27   Birth of a child, Elena Adelaide, registered in February as the Shelleys', allegedly at 250 Riviera di Chiaia. She may, among other possibilities, be a local child adopted by them or, less probably, CC's by PBS, Elise's by PBS or by someone else. When MWS first knows of the birth of Elena Adelaide, and how she feels about it, are unknown and, of course, would depend on which if any of these explanations is correct.

1819

January

Paolo Foggi is dismissed from the Shelleys' service for cheating them. At their insistence he marries Elise Duvillard, who is pregnant by him, and she leaves with him (see Journals, pp. 249–50, n3).

1   (Fri) In the evening the group are at the house of the Falconets – PBS's banker in Naples and his wife.

2   They go to the Studii again.

3   From now until 25 February MWS reads Sismondi's *Histoire des républiques italiennes du moyen âge*. Here she learns about Castruccio Castracani, about whom she will write in *Valperga*. She is also reading Dante's *Inferno* (until 20).

February

10   (Wed) They visit the palace of Caserta.

14   They visit Lago d'Agnano and the Grotto del Cane. Dr Roskilly, who is treating PBS for problems including pains in the side, dines with them.

23–25   They leave Naples briefly in order, via Salerno, to visit the temples at Paestum. On the way back on 25 they go to Pompeii again.

26   Another visit to the Studii.

27   Baptism of Elena Adelaide Shelley. (See 27 December
            1818.)
28   The Shelley group leaves Naples. Driven by Paolo Foggi's
            replacement, Vincenzo Gavita, they reach Capua on the
            first day.

March

1 (Mon) – 3 At Gaeta, where they play chess and stroll in the woods
            and by the sea. They continue to Terracina (3), Velletri
            (4) and, by way of the Alban Hills and Campagna, Rome
            (5). Here they stay first at the Villa di Parigi and then,
            from 7, at Palazzo Verospi on the Corso. MWS's manu-
            script tale 'Valerius, the Reanimated Roman' may be
            written in Rome this Spring.
8   The Shelleys and CC visit the Vatican Museum. On 9 the
            Shelleys are at the Villa Borghese (as often in the coming
            weeks) and, with CC, see the Pantheon and the
            Colosseum by moonlight. They go to the Capitol on 10
            and the Baths of Caracalla on 13, the Quirinal gardens
            on 17, the Tomb of Caius Cestius on 18, Palazzo Spada
            on 21, and many other well-known places.
11   They go to hear mass and the special sermon of the Padre
            Pacifico with the artist and writer Marianna Dionigi.
10 and 13   Frederick North, Lord Guildford, calls.
12   MWS sends Marianne Hunt an enthusiastic account of
            Rome; her life before it now seems a blank (Letters, i.89).
22   Dr John Bell calls; he comes again with his wife on 29.
            He will treat PBS and William.
24   MWS starts a course of drawing lessons.
28   The Shelleys and CC are at Marianna Dionigi's *conver-
            sazione*, as often on subsequent Sundays.

April

1 (Thurs)   MWS, PBS, and William visit the Vatican. In London *The
            New Monthly Magazine* 11, pp. 193–206, publishes
            Polidori's contribution to the ghost-story competition of
            June 1816 as 'The Vampyre: a Tale by Lord Byron'. A
            preface explains that it is not true, as rumour had it, that
            Byron had 'in his house two sisters as the partakers of his
            revels' in Switzerland – rather, Godwin's daughters 'Miss

M. W. Godwin and Miss Clermont' were with the atheist PBS. Between now and 16 Godwin takes action to have this and similar references removed from the book-length version of the account.

Having read *Hamlet* on 31 March, MWS reads *Romeo and Juliet, King Lear, Othello, Julius Caesar,* and *King John* between 1 and 5.

2 Emperor Francis I of Austria comes to Rome. MWS comments on his 'insolence' in a letter to Maria Gisborne on 9. She sees him again at the celebrations at the Capitol on 20.

8–11 The Shelleys and CC watch various Easter ceremonies.

9 By now MWS knows that she is pregnant again.

19 John Bell calls.

22 The Shelleys see the picture of Beatrice Cenci at Palazzo Colonna.

24 They go to the church of Trinità dei Monti and the Colosseum. In the evening they are visited by Italian musicians whom they have met at Marianna Dionigi's.

25 MWS reads the recently completed three-act version of PBS's *Prometheus Unbound.*

27 The Shelleys and CC have made contact with Amelia (or Aemilia) Curran, daughter of Godwin's close friend John Philpot Curran, who is studying and painting in Rome. They see her now almost daily. Several times at the end of this month and the beginning of next MWS mentions painting, probably under Curran's influence, rather than drawing, but soon resumes the latter activity.

May

7 (Fri) They move to 65 Via Sistina. Amelia Curran lives next door at 64. Originally they intended to set off on this date for Castellammare on the Bay of Naples, but have changed their minds because they now have friends in Rome and Curran is still working on her portraits of PBS and CC.

Between 7 and 22 MWS's reading includes Boccaccio's *Il Decamerone.*

11 The Shelleys and CC visit Palazzo Cenci.

13 To Tivoli with Amelia Curran.

14	Curran paints William. (The picture is at the Carl H. Pforzheimer Library.) PBS works on *The Cenci*; see 23–25 May 1818.
25	William is ill with worms. From 27 Dr Bell calls daily.
28	Curran paints MWS. (The picture is now lost.) William seems better.
30	MWS tells Maria Gisborne that, for various reasons but especially because William needs to be somewhere cooler, they are to leave Rome on 7 June and go probably to Bagni di Lucca.

June

2 (Wed)	William, still weak, falls ill again, this time with malaria. Dr Bell calls three times, but cannot save him. He dies on 7 and is buried in the Protestant Cemetery.
10	The grieving parents and CC leave Rome. MWS feels that she will never recover and blames the heat of Italy for the deaths of her children (Letters, i. 100, 101). She keeps no journal between 3 June and 4 August. They travel via Terni, Perugia and Arezzo to Livorno (17), where they stay at the Aquila Nera.
24	They move to the Villa Valsovano at Montenero, near Livorno. Here they often see the Gisbornes.

Some time between leaving Rome and early August MWS reads *Clarissa* in English (cp. April 1818).

July

15 (Thurs) Publication of Byron's *Don Juan*, Cantos One and Two.

August

MWS probably begins writing 'The Fields of Fancy' (re-named *Mathilda* by November). She is reading Dante's *Purgatorio* with PBS in the afternoons (until 20).

6 (Fri)	She reads Coleridge's *Remorse*.
	At mid-month she is copying PBS' *The Cenci*.
16	'Peterloo' massacre, in which a reform meeting in Manchester is broken up by cavalry, prompting PBS to write *The Mask of Anarchy*.
28	MWS starts on Dante's *Paradiso*, finishing it on 22 September.

September

4 (Sat)   Charles Clairmont joins the group at Montenero.

5–12   She finishes writing 'The Fields of Fancy' and makes the press transcript of Acts I–III of PBS's *Prometheus Unbound*. Between 9 and 23 she does the same for his *The Mask of Anarchy*.

23   PBS and Charles Clairmont go to Florence to arrange accommodation. They come back, PBS suffering from fever, on 25.

30   The Shelleys and Clairmonts travel to Pisa, where they meet Margaret King, Lady Mountcashell, now living with George Tighe and known as Mrs Mason. Mary Wollstonecraft was her governess.

October

1 (Fri)   They see Mrs Mason again and move on to Empoli.

2   The Shelleys, CC, and Charles Clairmont move into lodgings at Palazzo Marini, Via Valfonda, Florence.

11   They are at the Uffizi.

25   October – 2 November MWS copies PBS' *Peter Bell the Third*.

Late this month PBS works on 'Ode to the West Wind'.

November

9 (Tues)   MWS gives this date to *Mathilda*, the revised version of 'The Fields of Fancy', but probably does not finish correcting it until February 1820. She receives a letter from her father detailing his latest and most serious financial crisis: a lawsuit for back rent on the Skinner Street house has gone against him and he will soon be expected to pay £1500. As usual Godwin is convinced that PBS could bail him out, and there is some talk of his going to England in order to try to do so.

10   Charles Clairmont leaves for Vienna.

12   Birth of Percy Florence Shelley (1819–89).

December

MWS makes the press transcript of *Prometheus Unbound*, Act IV.
The Shelleys are in company with Mr and Mrs Meadows, fellow residents at Palazzo Marini, and a group including Sophia Stacey, a

young woman about whom PBS is much more enthusiastic than is MWS (Journals, p. 302 and n.3; Letters, i.118). Not knowing any Italians in Florence, MWS is having difficulty researching her novel about Castruccio Castracani (Letters i.120–1, n.4).

In mid-December Milly Shields leaves the Shelleys' employment.

28 (Tues)   MWS tells Maria Gisborne (Letters, i.121–2) about her enthusiasm for *The Faerie Queene.*

1820

January

3 (Mon)   PBS reads Byron's *Don Juan* cantos aloud. MWS continues reading them on 4 and goes on to his *Mazeppa* on 5.

5–23   She works on the translation of Spinoza's *Tractatus Theologico-politicus* which she and PBS began in 1817.

10   She is at the Pitti Palace with Mr Meadows. The Shelleys and CC continue often in the Meadows' company this month.

21   They go to the Gabinetto Fisico, a natural history museum, and on 22 to the Uffizi.

23   Elise Duvillard Foggi visits.

25   Percy Florence Shelley is baptized.

26   They travel by boat to Empoli and by carriage to Pisa, where at first they stay at the Tre Donzelle. (Walter Savage Landor is living in Pisa at this time but avoids meeting the Shelleys, he later confesses to MWS, because of a rumour about PBS's treatment of Harriet.)

27   They are with Mrs Mason, as often during their stay here.

29   Death of King George III and accession of George IV. The Shelleys and CC move into Casa Frassi.

31   Mrs Mason calls with her daughters, Laurette and Nerina.

31 – 2 February PBS is in Livorno.

February

11 (Thurs) Probable date on which MWS finishes correcting *Mathilda.*

20   Mrs Mason talks to the Shelleys and CC about the Irish rising of 1798, to one of the leaders of which she was related (Journals, pp. 309–10, n.3).

28 The Gisbornes visit, bringing with them the Shelleys' new servant, Caterina.

March

3 (Fri) – 6 PBS is in Livorno. Unknown to MWS, he is organizing payments connected with Elena Adelaide (Journals, p. 310, n.1).

4 MWS reads Tom Paine's *Common Sense*, on 5 his *Letter Addressed to the Abbé Raynal*, and then (5–11) his *Age of Reason*. Between 8 and 10 she reads Sir Thomas More's *Utopia*, and between 12 and 17 Paine's *Rights of Man*.

c. 6 She begins work on her novel about Castruccio Castracani.

9 The baby Percy has measles, but mildly, over the next fortnight or so.

10 News arrives of the foiled Cato Street Conspiracy against the British Cabinet.

14 The Shelleys and CC move to the more spacious top floor of Casa Frassi.

21 MWS and PBS take up the translation from Spinoza (see January). MWS works on it until 23 April.

26 MWS expresses, in a letter to Maria Gisborne, her support for the revolution in Spain which began in January; she would like to be in Madrid, she tells her in her next letter on 31.

31 Mrs Mason visits with her daughters Laurette and Nerina.

31 – 1 April She reads, in connection with her novel, Machiavelli's *La vita di Castruccio Castracani da Lucca*.

April

20 (Thurs) – 1 The Gisbornes visit. PBS goes back to Livorno with them, returning on 23.

21 Andrea Vaccà, the notable physician and liberal, a professor at the university of Pisa, calls. He is an old friend of the Gisbornes, and PBS has been advised by Mrs Mason to consult him about his health.

26 MWS is reading Ovid, probably *The Metamorphoses* since she is writing or about to write the mythological drama *Proserpine*.

28   The Shelleys are in Livorno to see the Gisbornes, who are
            bound for England.

27 – 11 May She reads Defoe's *Robinson Crusoe.*

May

3 (Wed)   She finishes *Proserpine.*

4   She reads Ovid again, presumably in preparation for
            writing her second mythological drama, *Midas*. (Like
            Proserpine, this contains some material by PBS.)

15–22   She reads Thomas Day's book for children, *Sandford
            and Merton.*

22–25   PBS goes to Livorno and Casciana, as on 10–11 June.

23–29   MWS reads Boswell's *Life of Johnson.*

June

1 (Thurs) – 7 She rereads works by her mother, and her father's
            Wollstonecraft *Memoirs.*

7   Arrival of a long-expected box from the Hunts. Its con-
            tents include baby clothes and three novels by Scott: *The
            Bride of Lammermoor*, *A Legend of Montrose* and *Ivanhoe*.
            Reading these (8–11) provides a new impetus in the
            writing of MWS's Castruccio Castracani novel (*Valperga*,
            ed. Curran, pp. xv–xviii).

8   'A better day than most' (Journals, p. 320); CC, between
            whom and MWS there is, as often before, tension, has
            gone away for the day.

9   Death in Naples of Elena Adelaide Shelley. News does
            not reach the Shelleys and CC until early in July.

12   Paolo Foggi attempts to blackmail the Shelleys, threat-
            ening to reveal 'facts' about Elena Adelaide's birth –
            probably that PBS and CC were the parents. On 13 PBS
            consults the lawyer Federico del Rosso in Livorno. PBS
            returns to Pisa on 14 and then on 15 moves, with the
            others, into the Gisbornes' house in Livorno, Casa
            Ricci. Del Rosso succeeds in forcing Foggi to desist. The
            adults suffer considerable stress and MWS believes that
            the baby is ill on 17 as a result of her feeding him
            while affected by it (Letters, i.147; Journals, p. 323
            and n.1).

18–20   She rereads Godwin's *Caleb Williams.*

30   Godwin writes to ask for a loan of £500. (See 9 November 1819 and Journals pp. 324–5, n.4.; PBS is increasingly dubious about the efficacy of lending or giving him money, and is himself seriously in debt.)

July

This month MWS reads several works by Cicero and begins to study Greek in earnest.

1 (Sat)   Revolution in Naples begins. Writing to Maria Gisborne on 19 she expresses the hope that other parts of Italy will follow the Neapolitan example.

18–20   CC stays with Mrs Mason in Pisa.

20   CC brings Laurette Mason to visit MWS.

20–25   PBS in Pisa.

29   PBS invites Keats to come to Italy.

August

This month and next MWS continues to work daily on Greek.

4 (Fri) – 5   The Shelleys and CC move to Casa Prinni, Bagni di San Giuliano, near Pisa.

10   MWS has written a story for Laurette (Journals, p. 328). The story, 'Maurice, or The Fisher's Cot' (rediscovered and identified in 1997), was probably written during the last few days (*Maurice*, ed. Tomalin, p. 147 n. 35).

11   The Shelleys and CC visit Lucca at the Croce di Malta. While PBS goes on to Monte San Pellegrino on 12 MWS and CC walk to sites in Lucca associated with Castruccio Castracani. They return to San Giuliano that evening, PBS on 13.

14   From now until 13 September she reads Ludovico Muratori's *Dissertazioni sopra le antichità italiane*.

14–16   She copies out PBS's *The Witch of Atlas*.

17   Queen Caroline's trial for adultery begins in the House of Lords.

c. 17   Publication of PBS's *Prometheus Unbound: a Lyrical Drama in Four Acts, with Other Poems*.

24   Mrs Mason visits.

31   PBS escorts CC to Livorno, where she stays in the Gisbornes' house. Sea-bathing has been recommended

for her health, and friction between her and MWS makes their separation increasingly desirable.

September

1 (Fri) – 8	MWS reads several books on Irish history.
3	PBS arrives back from Livorno.
4, 12, 18	The Shelleys go into Pisa. On 6, 10, and 15 they go for mountain walks.
16	Mrs Mason visits.
20	Between now and 23 November MWS records 'Write' almost every day in her Journal (except when interrupted at the end of October and beginning of November). She is working on the Castruccio novel (*Valperga*).
22	Vaccà calls.

October

1 (Sun)	PBS goes to Livorno and brings CC back to San Giuliano. By 5 she has gone to stay with Mrs Mason in Pisa, returning a few days later.
c. 5	The Gisbornes return to Livorno from England.
10 and 12	The Shelleys are in Pisa again. On 13 they visit Vico Pisano.
14	MWS re-reads the two *Don Juan* cantos so far published.
16	She goes to Livorno to see the Gisbornes, between whom and the Shelleys a rift has developed as a result of accusations – mainly about financial matters and Allegra's paternity – made in conversations at Skinner Street. On 17 PBS delivers to Livorno an angry letter from MWS. Reconciliation will be achieved only next summer.
17	She reads *Prometheus Unbound*.
18	PBS reads *Hyperion* aloud from Keats's *Lamia, Isabella, The Eve of St. Agnes, and Other Poems*. MWS continues to read the volume the next day.
20	PBS goes to Florence with CC. On 21 she takes up residence as a paying guest in the house of the Bojti family.
21	MWS rides to Pisa.
22	PBS arrives back at San Giuliano, bringing with him from Pisa his cousin, Thomas Medwin.

25   The house is flooded when the nearby canal bursts its banks after heavy rainfall. An inflammation of the eyes also helps to prevent MWS working over the next few days.

29   The Shelleys, with Medwin, move into Palazzo Galetti, Pisa.

November

5 (Sun) – 6 Henry Reveley visits.

13   The eye inflammation returns and, briefly it seems, keeps her 'from all study' (Journals, p. 340).

14   MWS starts learning Spanish.

21   CC arrives in Pisa and stays until 23 December.

24   News arrives of the abandonment of the case against Queen Caroline (see 17 August). First visit of Francesco Pacchiani, eccentric and spellbinding professor of various subjects at the university of Pisa and a possible inspiration for Battista Tripalda in *Valperga* (Seymour, p. 262). The Shelleys and CC will soon come to dislike him.

December

Beginning this month, mainly through the friends and contacts of Dr Vaccà and his wife, the Shelleys and CC enter Pisan social life. As well as Pacchiani, they meet the *improvvisatore* Tommaso Sgricci, the minor Irish poet and Dante commentator John Taaffe, professor of law Ferdinando Foggi, Prince Alexandros Mavrokordatos (soon to become one of the Greek leaders in the war for independence from the Turks) and his cousin Princess Ralou Argyropoulo. MWS becomes especially close to Mavrokordatos, with whom she studies Greek and discusses the hopes for Greek independence. They also see Mrs Mason and frequently visit Teresa Viviani, daughter of the Governor of Pisa, whose family have sent her to live at the convent of Sant'Anna and whom they call 'Emilia'. PBS's enthusiasm for her is greater and longer lasting than MWS's and may contribute to her perceived coldness towards him at this time.

21 (Thurs) The Shelleys and CC attend, and are much impressed and delighted by, a performance by Sgricci. He improvises on the stories of Pyramus and Thisbe and Iphigeneia in Aulis.

23   CC returns to Florence.

In late 1820 or early 1821 MWS writes 'The Necessity of a Belief in the Heathen Mythology to a Christian', a manuscript answer to Charles Leslie's *Short and Easy Method With the Deists* (1820).

1821

January

5 (Fri)   MWS sees Sgricci perform in Lucca. On 11 she goes there again, accompanied by Pacchiani since PBS is ill, watches Sgricci on 12, and returns to Pisa on 13. She watches him again on 22, when his subject is the Death of Hector.

19   Medwin introduces Edward and Jane Williams to the Shelleys. At once they become good friends and see each other most days. Edward is particularly close to MWS and Jane to PBS.

21   The Shelleys and Williamses are at the opera.

26   Possible date (Nora Crook, ed., *The 'Charles the First' Draft Notebook*, 1991, p. xli) for work on 'Orpheus', a fragmentary poem possibly co-written by MWS and PBS.

28 and 29   Henry Reveley visits.

February

PBS writes *Epipsychidion*, addressed to Emilia Viviani. MWS does not see the poem until the summer.

1 (Thurs)   Reveley calls again.

2   The Shelleys and Williamses go to a performance of Cimarosa's *Il matrimonio segreto*.

6–8   MWS sits for a portrait (not extant) by Edward Williams.

6   When Mavrokordatos visits there is 'a long metaphysical argument' (Journals, p. 352).

10, 12   MWS reads Dante's *La vita nuova*.

17   A day representative of some of her main activities at this time: she works at Greek, rides with Mrs Mason, walks with Edward Williams, and sees Mavrokordatos in the evening.

23   The Shelleys ride to the Bagni di San Giuliano with the Williamses.

27   Medwin leaves for Rome. He has been with the Shelleys since October 1820. MWS finds him dull.

March

The Shelleys continue to call on Emilia Viviani on many occasions this spring.

5 (Mon)   The Shelleys move to new lodgings at Casa Aulla.

11–12   MWS finishes Sidney's *A Defence of Poesie*, which she began on 1. Between 12 and 20 she transcribes PBS's *A Defence of Poetry*.

16   Birth of the Williamses' daughter Rosalind. News of the (abortive) revolution in Piedmont arrives. On 18 comes news of the defeat of the Neapolitan rebels by the Austrians.

25   To the opera with Edward Williams and Laurette Mason.

April

1 (Sun)   Mavrokordatos is 'as gay as a caged eagle just free' (Journals, p. 359) because the Greeks have proclaimed their independence. Probably at MWS's suggestion, he stops teaching her Greek so that he can give more time to the cause.

2   The Shelleys go to hear the tenor Niccolo Tachinardi.

10–14   MWS is reading Marco Lastri's *L'osservatore fiorentino sugli edifizi della sua patria*. On 17 she sends Hunt an extract from it – an account of a sixteenth-century duel – hoping that he will be able to use it in *The Indicator* (which, unknown to her, has ceased publication).

11   The Shelleys learn that Keats died in Rome on 23 February.

15   PBS, Reveley, and Edward Williams go to Livorno to inspect PBS's new small boat. They try to sail back to Pisa by canal but capsize. PBS and Williams arrive home the following day.

26–30   The Gisbornes visit. A degree of cordiality has been re-established.

May

5 (Sat)   Death of Napoleon.

8   Mavrokordatos and MWS walk to Pugnano to see the Williamses. The Shelleys move back to the Bagni di San Giuliano. From here, as before, they often go into Pisa. Contact with the Williamses remains close and PBS and Edward Williams often go sailing together.

11	Another period of work on the Castruccio novel begins.
21	Mavrokordatos visits San Giuliano.

June

2 (Sat)	MWS walks to Pisa with Williams.
14–17, 25	She is reading plays, probably in Scott's *The Ancient English Drama* (see Journals, p. 370 n.1.) Between 18 and 23 she reads Malthus's *Essay on the Principle of Population* and on 23–24 Godwin's reply to it, *Of Population* ....
21	They see CC, who is visiting Mrs Mason. She goes to stay in Livorno on 23.
22	MWS calls on Emilia Viviani in Pisa, probably for the last time, and on Princess Argyropoulo and her husband, before dining with Mrs Mason.
25–26	The Shelleys are worried when their son Percy has a fever, but he soon recovers. PBS is also ill and Vaccà calls several times.
26	Mavrokordatos sails for Greece.
28	They go to Pugnano in the boat.
30	MWS reports to Maria Gisborne that she is at last making good progress with the Castruccio novel.

July

Emilia Viviani, who is to marry in September, asks the Shelleys to end their visits to her. She will be an inspiration for Clorinda in MWS's 'The Bride of Modern Italy' (see April 1824).

MWS's reading again includes the collection of 'Old Plays'.

5 (Thurs)	Between now and June 1822 she reads *The Odyssey*.
10	Hunt has rejected a story (still unidentified) intended by MWS for *The Indicator*.
12	She reads PBS's *Adonais*.
17	Mrs Mason calls. CC stays with her again during 21–27 and comes to San Giuliano on 23. They are with CC again in Pisa on 25 and she returns to Livorno on 27.
21	Publication in Paris of Jules Saladin's translation *Frankenstein, ou le Prométhée moderne*.
26–29	The Gisbornes visit. They are soon to return to England.
28	MWS reads part of the draft version of her novel to Maria Gisborne.
29 – 2 August	PBS is in Florence.

30   MWS sits for Williams again. He finishes his picture on 4 August.

August

3   (Fri) PBS sets off to see Byron in Ravenna, pausing to visit CC in Livorno.

6   She reads *Mathilda* to Williams. PBS arrives in Ravenna.

7   PBS has learnt from Byron that the Hoppners have believed and repeated Elise Foggi's claim that Elena was CC's child by PBS. On 10, at PBS's request, MWS addresses to Mrs Hoppner an indignant letter denying the allegation, professing her love for PBS and the impossibility of his or CC having behaved in such a way, and attacking the Hoppners for crediting the tale. It is possible, however, that Byron fails to forward the letter to them.

          Some time after 7 MWS begins copying the near-final version of the novel, which she intends to call *Castruccio, Prince of Lucca*.

8   Publication of Byron's *Don Juan*, Cantos III–V.

11   Encouraged by PBS, Byron has decided that he and Teresa Guiccioli will move to Pisa. PBS writes to ask MWS to look for a suitable house for them.

17   CC comes to stay at San Giuliano (until 27). She and MWS see Edward Williams every morning.

22   PBS arrives home from Ravenna.

Towards the end of the month Teresa Guiccioli and her father and brother, the Counts Gamba, settle in Pisa.

September

1 (Sat)   Teresa Guiccioli meets MWS for the first time. They see each other again on 5 and regular contact begins.

4   MWS reads *Mathilda* to Jane Williams.

5–15   CC stays with the Shelleys.

6   MWS reads Scott's *Kenilworth*.

7   She finishes copying the penultimate draft of *Castruccio*.

8   The Shelleys and CC go to La Spezia. They go out on the Bay on 9 and are in Massa and Carrara on 10 before returning to San Giuliano on 11.

15   They go to Vico Pisano, as described in 'Recollections of
            Italy' (*Collected Tales*, pp. 29–30; see below, January 1824.)
On 17 the Shelleys go to Pisa with the Williamses and on 18 picnic
with them 'on the Pugnano mountain'.

October
MWS copies or revises the final version of *Castruccio*.
9 (Tues) – 11 CC stays with the Shelleys in San Giuliano. She then
            stays with the Williamses at Pugnano until 30 and
            briefly with Mrs Mason in Pisa.
10 (Wed)   Godwin says that 'Maurice' is too short to publish.
25   The Shelleys move into rooms on the top floor of the Tre
            Palazzi di Chiesa in Pisa.

November
1 (Thurs)   CC goes to live in Florence again in order to avoid
            Byron, who today moves into Palazzo Lanfranchi, across
            the Arno from Tre Palazzi di Chiesa. During their
            months together in Pisa MWS is often with Guiccioli but
            sees rather less of Byron than does PBS.
2   MWS reads Byron's soon-to-be-published *Cain*, which
            is, she tells Maria Gisborne on 30, 'in the highest style
            of imaginative Poetry' (Letters, i.209).
4–24   The Williamses live with the Shelleys before moving
            downstairs to a lower floor of the Tre Palazzi.
9   MWS reads the manuscript of Byron's *The Vision of
            Judgement*.
By 11 MWS has completed *Castruccio, Prince of Lucca*. Some revision
            is still needed; she notes that she is correcting the novel
            from 30 and finishes it on 3 December, probably reading
            aloud to Jane Williams as she works (Journals, p. 384
            n. 3). She hopes that it will be published before
            Christmas but Charles Ollier shows no interest. (See 19
            February 1823.)
14   Medwin comes to Pisa (until about 10 March 1822).

December
7 (Fri)   The Shelleys buy furniture for the Hunts, who are
            expected to arrive soon and move into part of Palazzo

	Lanfranchi, but have, as yet unknown to the Shelleys, been turned back by bad weather in the English Channel.
9	MWS goes to a service conducted by Rev. George Frederick Nott in his rooms in the Tre Palazzi. She goes again, for the christening of her godchild Rosalind Williams, on 30. Subsequently Nott speaks against atheists but, in response to MWS's letter of complaint, denies that he meant to attack PBS individually.
12–20	She reads Scott's *Ivanhoe*, *Waverley*, *The Antiquary* and *Rob Roy*.
26	They are at the opera to hear the tenor John Sinclair.

1822

This year at Pisa, according to Edward John Trelawny, Byron wanted to perform *Othello* with himself as Iago, Trelawny as Othello, and MWS as Desdemona (Letters, i.470, n.7). This idea probably pre-dates the Masi affair (see 24 March).

January

13 (Sun) – 15	MWS is rereading Rousseau's *Emile*.
13	The Shelleys are at the opera with the Williamses, Pietro Gamba, and the sculptor Lorenzo Bartolini. There are further evenings at the opera on 15, 17,19, 27, and 29.
14	Trelawny's first meeting with the Shelleys. He has come to Pisa as a friend of Medwin and the Williamses, and wishing to meet PBS and Byron. His knowledge of boats and sailing appeals instantly to PBS and Edward Williams.
16	While the men dine at Byron's, MWS dines with Jane Williams and reads her his *Werner*. Between 17 and 25 she fair-copies it for him.
19	MWS writes in her journal her early impressions of Trelawny: his physical attractiveness, good nature, horrific stories told in simple but strong language; unlike most people, he interests her imagination (Journals, p. 391).
23	Trelawny introduces MWS to Mrs Emily Jane Beauclerk, a neighbour of PBS's family in Sussex and one of the few members of the expatriate English community willing to

	receive her, particularly since the scandal excited by Dr Nott's sermon (see 9 December 1821).
24	MWS reads Byron's *Sardanapalus* and on 26 *The Two Foscari*.
28	The Shelleys and Jane Williams go to the mouth of the Arno in PBS's small boat.
30 – 2 February MWS reads Scott's *The Pirate*.	

February

2 (Sat)	The Shelleys and Jane Williams walk through the Cascine pine-forest to the sea.
5–12	MWS continues reading *Emile*.
7–11	PBS and Edward Williams househunt in La Spezia.
7	MWS goes to the opera with Trelawny and Jane Williams and afterwards to a ball given by Emily Beauclerk. MWS is highly stimulated by Trelawny's company at this time. On 8 she and Jane are again fascinated by his stories and on 9 she manages to 'retire' with him (Journals, p. 397) from more tedious company to hear more of the same. The two women go to the opera with him again on 10 and continue to see him most days.
17 and 19	She is at the Veglione or masked ball, probably in Turkish dress (Journals, p. 398, n. 4).
21–25	CC comes to Pisa. The Shelleys dissuade her from going to live in Vienna.
24	After church MWS calls on Emily Beauclerk.

March

She continues often in the company of Trelawny, the Williamses, Guiccioli, Beauclerk, and sometimes Mrs Mason. She sees Byron on 4, 8, and 12.

1 (Fri)	She starts with a new Greek teacher.
9	She goes to the opera to see Johann Simon Mayr's *Ginevra di Scozia*.
11–12	She reads Lady Morgan's *Florence Macarthy*.
17	The Shelleys write to CC to persuade her that it is impossible for them to try further to influence Byron over the fate of Allegra.
21	The Shelleys and Williamses sail on the Arno and then see an Italian version of Voltaire's *Histoire de Charles X* (Journals, p. 403, n. 1).

| 24 | Scandal and confusion follow a scuffle between Sergeant-Major Stefano Masi and a group including PBS, Byron, and Pietro Gamba. For a time it is expected that Masi will die from a wound inflicted by one of Byron's servants. On 25 MWS visits the hospital where the wounded man is being treated. |
| 31 | By about this date she knows that she is pregnant again (Journals, p. 406, n. 3). |

April

4 (Thurs) – 21	She reads Machiavelli's *Historie Fiorentine*.
13	She rides to San Giuliano.
15	CC comes to stay.
19 or 20	Death of Allegra, of typhus, at Bagnacavallo. (On the date see *Maurice*, ed. Tomalin, pp. 147–8, n. 41.)
19	MWS makes a statement to the authorities about the Masi affair.
23	News of Allegra's death reaches the Shelleys while CC is with the Williamses in La Spezia. She returns to Pisa on 25. The Shelleys break the news to her only on 2 May.
26	MWS, CC, Trelawny, and Percy Florence set off for La Spezia, where they intend to spend the summer. They sleep at Massa. On 27–28 they househunt in La Spezia, where Trelawny leaves the others on 28. On 29 they are at Sarzana and engage the Villa Magni at San Terenzo, near Lerici, into which, joined by PBS, they move on 30. The Williamses arrive and move in with them soon afterwards.

May

This month MWS re-reads Tasso's *Gerusalemme liberata*. Letters from Godwin insistently demand money and it is agreed that Mrs Mason and PBS will in future vet the contents before passing them on to MWS. Much of the time at the Villa Magni she is deeply depressed. This 'dungeon', as she calls it on about 30 June (to Hunt, Letters i. 238), is remote, next to the roaring sea; she hates the natives and their dialect and even natural beauty makes her shudder and weep (Letters i. 244). Communication with her husband all but ceases. He finds the company of Jane Williams easier.

| 12 (Sun) | PBS takes possession of his new boat, the *Don Juan*. |
| 21 | CC goes back to Florence and soon afterwards to Pisa. |

June

1 (Sat) and 5   MWS goes out in the *Don Juan*; only on the water, with her eyes closed and her head on PBS's knee, does she feel at peace (Letters, i. 244). PBS and Edward Williams use it for several longer expeditions, for example to Viareggio on 6–7.

7   CC returns to the Villa Magni.

9   MWS nearly miscarries.

At some point between 12 of this month and 7 July she reads Ugo Foscolo's *Ultime lettere di Jacopo Ortis*.

13–16   Trelawny visits.

16   MWS miscarries and almost dies from loss of blood. PBS saves her by making her sit in ice.

18   PBS tells John Gisborne that Italy delights him but he feels the lack of someone 'who can feel, and understand me. Whether from proximity and the continuity of domestic intercourse, Mary does not' (PBS Letters, ii.715). On the night of 23 and other occasions, still very weak, she is further depressed by PBS's tormenting nightmares and visions.

26   The Godwins move to 195 The Strand.

July

The Hunts have at last arrived in Italy. On 1 (Mon) PBS and Edward Williams sail the *Don Juan* to Livorno and see them on 2. PBS then visits Byron and Mrs Mason in Pisa.

8   PBS, Williams, and the boat-boy Charles Vivian sail from Livorno but are drowned in a squall soon after setting out.

12   MWS and Jane Williams discover that their husbands set off for home on 8. Desperate for news of them, they go first to Pisa to ask Byron and Guiccioli and then to Livorno, early on 13, to ask Trelawny, who accompanies them back to the Villa Magni.

18   Trelawny discovers that the bodies have been washed ashore. He comes to the Villa Magni to inform the widows on 19, bringing MWS some comfort by the eloquence of his tribute to PBS.

20   Trelawny takes the widows and CC back to the Tre Palazzi in Pisa.

29   MWS tells Medwin that she feels PBS is alive and often with her, that his elemental spirit is now free of its

earthly prison. She hopes to be worthy to join him, but in the meantime her life will be one of 'study only – Except for my poor boy' (Letters, i.243).

August

15 (Thurs) Trelawny, accompanied by Hunt, Byron, and others, supervises the cremation of Edward Williams at Migliarino, followed on 16 by that of PBS near Viareggio. Until now their bodies have been buried in the sand with quicklime to fulfil local health requirements. The women remain in Pisa. Hunt takes possession of PBS's heart and for some days withholds it from MWS.

25 She goes to Livorno to see the box containing PBS's ashes. In September it is sent to Rome, where it is eventually buried in the Protestant cemetery in January 1823.

c. 27 In a letter to Maria Gisborne MWS mentions the idea of collecting PBS's manuscripts and writing his life. (She has already requested manuscripts in Peacock's possession.) She also reports that she sees Trelawny, whom she still finds particularly helpful and sympathetic, about once a week, Byron and Guiccioli about twice a week, and Mrs Mason, whom she finds surprisingly cold towards her, about every ten days.

30 MWS's twenty-fifth birthday.

September

Between the beginning of the month and 10 she fair-copies Cantos VI–IX of *Don Juan*.

11 (Wed) MWS and Jane Williams travel with Trelawny to Genoa, where they stay at the Croce di Malta. (CC remains in Pisa until 15, when she goes to Florence.) MWS is to find a house for herself and the Hunts to rent; on about 25 she moves into Casa Negroto, Albaro, at £40 a year, of which she takes it upon herself to pay at least half. Byron, Guiccioli, and the Gambas are to live about a mile away at Casa Saluzzi.

17 Jane Williams and her children set off for England. In Pisa she told Hunt that MWS was responsible for PBS's unhappiness, and this will add uneasiness to the relationship between MWS and the Hunts in Genoa.

20   CC sets off to join her brother Charles in Vienna, where she remains until moving to Russia to work as a governess in 1824.

In Genoa MWS works on *The Liberal*, the magazine owned and written mainly by Byron and Hunt, and originally PBS's idea. The first number goes to the printer on 29. One of her tasks is to copy suitable work by PBS for this and subsequent numbers.

October

MWS begins a new 'Journal of Sorrow', written mainly when she can be alone at night. Entries frequently explore her grief, loneliness, and, as others misperceive it, coldness (see e.g. Journals, p. 444).

3 (Thurs)   Byron, Guiccioli, and Trelawny arrive in Genoa.
4   The Hunts arrive at Casa Negroto.
5   Her task in life apart from caring for her son Percy, she feels, will be to commemorate the virtues of PBS (Journals, p. 434).
15   The first number of *The Liberal* is published.
19   Having spent two hours with Byron she wonders why his voice has such a powerful effect on her and decides that it is because she expects to hear PBS reply.
21   She has nearly finished copying Canto XI of *Don Juan*.

November

6 (Wed)   She has recently finished writing 'A Tale of the Passions', begun at some point before the death of PBS (see 1 January 1823).
14   Byron sends her part of *The Deformed Transformed* to copy.
17   She expresses in her journal the intention of writing PBS's life. (See 10 February 1823 and March 1823.)
22   MWS again tells Maria Gisborne that she is keen to gather together PBS's manuscripts from all possible sources.

December

Trelawny, whom MWS has seen often over the last few months, leaves Genoa until June 1823.

7 (Sat)–12 She fair-copies *Don Juan*, Canto XII.
19   She is copying Edward Williams's journal, which was recovered from the wreck of the *Don Juan*.

1823

Before 1824 MWS writes a fragmentary story called by Robinson 'An Eighteenth Century Tale: a Fragment' (*Collected Tales*, pp. 345–6). Possibly at about the same time she writes 'The Heir of Mondolfo', a story which remains unpublished until 1877.

January
She re-reads Sidney's *Arcadia*, recommending its 'exquisite sentiments and descriptions' to Jane Williams on 12 (Letters, i.305).

1 (Wed)   MWS's anonymous 'A Tale of the Passions, or, the Death of Despina' appears in *The Liberal*, vol. 2, pp. 289–325. From the first two numbers of *The Liberal* she earns either £33 or £36 (see Letters, i.310, n.3). Later this year the story is serialized in *The Weekly Entertainer; and West of England Miscellany*, n.s. 7.

By 10 she is copying Byron's *The Age of Bronze*.

12   She asks Godwin, through Jane Williams, to send her some books for Percy, including Anna Laetitia Barbauld's *Lessons for Children* and Wollstonecraft's *Original Stories*.

25   Byron sends MWS more scenes of *The Deformed Transformed* to copy. When she returns the manuscript a week later she urges him to complete this work which, she feels, is equal to anything he has written (Letters, i.311; *Collected Tales*, p. 381, considers the work as a source for MWS's story 'Transformation', published in late 1830). She is displeased, however, that he will not send money to CC, who is ill in Vienna; he is prepared only to lend the money to MWS, who is determined not to borrow from him. She herself sends money to CC. She changes her mind several times this summer about Byron's true personal worth or lack of it.

February
10 (Mon)   She dates the first part of her fragmentary life of PBS either today or 10 February 1824.

19   Publication by G. and W. B. Whittaker of MWS's *Valperga: or, the Life and Adventures of Castruccio, Prince of Lucca*, by 'the Author of *Frankenstein*'. The title is Godwin's; having failed to persuade Charles Ollier to

publish the novel, the Shelleys sent it to Godwin to place elsewhere at the end of 1821. Other alterations are probably fairly minimal, except that he cuts details of the battles after the death of Beatrice. (See *Letters*, i.323–4, n.10.) Many reviews of the novel criticize its narrative structure while praising 'eloquence, sentiment, painterly qualities and characters (except for Castruccio's)' (*Novels and Selected Works*, 3.xiv). Comparisons with *Frankenstein* vary from pleased recognition of 'the same wild imagination' in *The Literary Gazette* to relief at finding 'a more sober turn of feeling' in *The Ladies' Monthly Museum*. The review in *Knight's Quarterly Magazine* for August 1824 speculates that either PBS wrote *Frankenstein* or, since *Valperga* doesn't read like his work, MWS 'wrote Frankenstein – but, knowing that its fault was extravagance, determined to be careful and correct it in her next work; and thence, as so many do from the same cause, became commonplace'.

24   By now she has probably finished fair-copying *Don Juan*, Canto XIII. Byron (PBS's executor, with Peacock) sends her Sir Timothy Shelley's reply to his enquiries about provision for herself and Percy: he will give her nothing and will provide for Percy only if he is placed in the care of someone of his choosing. Byron later angers MWS by suggesting she should agree to this course of action.

March

Either this month or in March 1824 she continues, but soon abandons, her life of PBS.

30 (Sun)   By now she has probably finished fair-copying *Don Juan*, Canto XV she assures Byron that the task delights her and asks whether Aurora Raby is 'a portrait'.

April

Byron, advising MWS to return to England, says that he will pay her travelling expenses. They are on good terms again. In the end, however, she does not receive the money (see June).

26 (Sat)   MWS's essay 'Madame D'Houtetot' is published in *The Liberal*, vol. 3, pp. 67–83.

May

She decides to go to England once Marianne Hunt has had the baby she is expecting (the Hunts' seventh child, Vincent, born on 9 June). Although she would prefer to stay in Italy she feels that her and Percy's presence may influence Sir Timothy Shelley and others in their favour. She also wants her child to avoid the heat of an Italian summer.

21 (Wed) By now she has finished fair-copying Canto XVI of *Don Juan*.

June

Relations between MWS and Byron become strained. She refuses to take money from him for her journey and is helped instead by Trelawny and Margaret Mason. Byron offends MWS by remarks, of exactly what nature is unclear, to Hunt about her and PBS. Byron does, however, unknown to MWS, attempt to pay her passage through Hunt, who keeps the money for himself. (Seymour, p. 325 and n.50.)

July

Early this month Guiccioli attempts, with limited success, to effect a reconciliation between MWS and Byron. By now MWS and Hunt are friends again.

About now she gives a friend of Trelawny in Genoa, Mrs Thomas, a copy of *Frankenstein* with corrections (now at the Pierpont Morgan Library, New York).

MWS gives this month as the date of her poem 'The Choice'.

17 (Thurs) Byron, Trelawny, and Pietro Gamba sail for Greece. MWS visits Teresa Guiccioli.

25 MWS and Percy Florence set off for England. They are at Asti on 26 and proceed to Turin (27), Susa (28), St Jean de la Maurienne (30), and Chambéry (31).

28 Richard Brinsley Peake's *Presumption; or, the Fate of Frankenstein* opens at the English Opera House (or – its earlier and later name – the Lyceum) for a run of thirty-seven performances.

30 Her essay 'Giovanni Villani' appears in *The Liberal*, vol. 4, pp. 281–97. This is the final issue of the periodical.

August

1 (Fri) MWS and Percy reach Pont Bon Voisin. They stay at Lyon (2–5) and are at Dijon on 7 and Auxerre by 9.

5	She is considering writing a novel about Alfred the Great.

| 11 | The second edition of *Frankenstein* is published at 14s. by G. and W. B. Whittaker, as the work of Mary Wollstonecraft Shelley. 250–500 copies are printed. Godwin has arranged publication and is very probably responsible for minor alterations; see *Novels and Selected Works*, 1.xcvi-xcvii. News that *Presumption* was about to be put on suggested the timing of the edition; see *Letters*, i.379, and *Novels and Selected Works*, p. xcvi. |

12   MWS and Percy reach Paris, where they stay at the Hôtel Nelson.

14   Horace Smith calls. He and his family are living at Versailles, where she visits them between 15 and 18. Here she enjoys the company of the playwright James Kenney, his wife Louisa, widow of Godwin's friend Thomas Holcroft, and her daughter Louisa Holcroft. They see her again on 19.

18   Henry Milner's *Frankenstein; or, the Demon of Switzerland* opens at the Royal Coburg Theatre for eight performances. (See also 3 July 1826.)

20   MWS and Percy travel from Paris to Calais.

25   They reach London and stay with the Godwins.

29   MWS goes to see *Presumption* with Godwin, William Godwin Jr., and Jane Williams. MWS feels that 'the story is not well managed', but admires Thomas Potter Cooke's performance as the monster. There is 'a breathless eagerness' in the audience (*Letters*, i.378).

30   She sees the Gisbornes and Charles Lamb.

September

1 (Mon)   *Hungumption; or Dr Frankenstein and the Hobgoblin of Hoxton* opens at the New Surrey Theatre. There are six performances. *Presumption and the Blue Demon* is performed twice at Davis's Royal Amphitheatre.

3 (Wed)   With her father she sees Sir Timothy Shelley's lawyer, William Whitton, who gives her £100 for expenses and the promise of £100 a year for her son. She also at last sees her old friend Isabel Baxter Booth.

8   MWS and Percy move to 14 Speldhurst Street, Brunswick Square, London.

10   She meets Leigh Hunt's brother, the publisher John
          Hunt, for the first time. On 18, writing to Leigh Hunt,
          she says that John has agreed to publish her PBS manu-
          scripts. She has been approached to write the preface but
          would rather it came from Leigh Hunt.

          Some time between 10 and 18 MWS meets the poet and
          PBS enthusiast Bryan Waller Procter (Barry Cornwall).
          Probably soon afterwards she meets the poet Thomas
          Lovell Beddoes.

19   She goes to Richmond to watch Marianne Hunt's
          brother, the actor Tom Kent.

25   She dines with the Novello family at Shacklewell Green.

October

4 (Sat)   She is at the Novellos' again, with Jane Williams, the
          Lambs, Charles Cowden Clarke, and others. As usual
          there is much music; ideas for writing, she tells Leigh
          Hunt on 5, rise and develop when she listens to music,
          especially now instrumental music. She also tells Hunt
          that she is working on a piece for the *London Magazine*
          (see January, March, and April 1824), has given up the
          notion of a novel about King Alfred, and intends to write
          something 'more wild & imaginative' – possibly she has
          ideas by now for *The Last Man*.

19   She is at the Novellos' with her half-brother William,
          Jane Williams, and musicians. She visits the Lambs on
          about 23, the Novellos again on 25.

20   Richard Brinsley Peake's burlesque *Another Piece of
          Presumption* opens at the Adelphi Theatre for nine
          performances.

28   She is at the Gisbornes' with Hogg and Jane Williams.
          She also sees Peacock sometimes.

November

She is gathering and editing material for PBS's *Posthumous Poems*.

15   MWS and the Novellos are at the Lambs'.

17   Ninety-two copies of *Six Weeks' Tour* remain unsold (see
          Letters i.401).

26   The diarist Henry Crabb Robinson is at the Godwins' with
          the Lambs and MWS. 'She is unaltered', says Robinson,

who has presumably not seen her for some years, 'yet I did not know her at first; she looks elegant and sickly and young. One would not suppose she was the author [of *Frankenstein*]' (*On Books and their Writers*, p. 299).

27 and 28   She visits the British Museum.

December

4 (Thurs)   MWS and the Godwins go to a production of *The Winter's Tale* with the American playwright John Howard Payne, whom MWS has met recently at the Godwins'.

9 and 10   She sees John Hunt. (She, Vincenzo Novello and other friends are trying to mediate between the brothers in their complicated dispute over their rights and finances in *The Examiner*.)

13   Godwin recommends MWS to Henry Colburn as a suitable contributor to his *New Monthly Magazine*.

1824

This year there are revivals of the *Frankenstein* adaptation *Presumption* at the English Opera House and Covent Garden.

January

MWS's 'Recollections of Italy' is published anonymously in the *London Magazine*, vol. 9, pp. 21–6.

13 (Tues)   Godwin sends Colburn an article by MWS (not certainly identified) for possible inclusion in the *New Monthly Magazine*.

17 or 18   She sees Coleridge, probably at the Lambs' (Journal, p. 474 and n.2). His 'beautiful descriptions, metaphysical talk & subtle distinctions' remind her of PBS's conversation and her daily contact with one who was actively good and whose 'wild picturesque mode of living ... suited my active spirit & satisfied its craving for novelty of impression'.

26   With the Godwins she sees Kean as Richard III at Drury Lane; she sees him as Shylock on 31.

February

8 (Fri) She sees the Lambs.

9 She tells Hunt that, inspired by watching Kean recently at Drury Lane, she is attempting to write a tragedy. She also intends to plunge into writing a novel; she is perhaps about to start work on *The Last Man*.

13 MWS, Jane Williams, and Hogg go to the theatre, probably to see Kean as Sir Giles Overreach in Massinger's *A New Way to Pay Old Debts* at Drury Lane. She 'was never more powerfully affected by any representation', she writes to Trelawny (Letters, i.416).

27 Godwin, having read his daughter's sample scenes for a tragedy, tells her that they are too abstract and that she is clearly no dramatist.

March

Publication of MWS's essay 'On Ghosts' in the *London Magazine*, vol. 9, pp. 281–97.

16 (Tues) George Canning, the Foreign Secretary, alludes to *Frankenstein* in a House of Commons debate: to free West Indian slaves 'would be to raise up a creature resembling the splendid fiction of a recent romance, the hero of which constructs a human form, with all the corporeal capabilities of man, and with the thews and sinews of a giant; but being unable to impart to the work of his hands a perception of right and wrong, he finds too late that he has only created a more than mortal power of doing mischief, and himself recoils from the monster which he has made'.

April

MWS's 'The Bride of Modern Italy' is published anonymously in the *London Magazine*, vol. 9, pp. 351–63.

19 (Mon) Death of Byron at Missolonghi.

May

9 (Sun) MWS sends *Proserpine* and *Midas* to Bryan Waller Procter in hope of publication.

14 She feels friendless, longs for Italy, and fears that her intellectual powers are failing; 'The last man! Yes I may

	well describe that solitary being's feelings, feeling myself as the last relic of a beloved race, my companions, extinct before me' (*Journals*, pp. 476–7). By now she is working on *The Last Man*.
15	She hears the news of Byron's death. On 16 she sends a letter of condolence to Teresa Guiccioli. Probably in the last week of the month (*Letters*, i.422 and 423 n.2), she sends a tribute to him to the *London Magazine* but it is not published and remains lost.
25	John Howard Payne sends MWS tickets for his *Charles the Second* at Covent Garden. She is unable to go, but takes advantage of his offers on many subsequent occasions. He falls in love with her over the coming months. She likes him but does not reciprocate his love. (See 25 July 1825.)

June

Early in the month John Hunt publishes 500 copies of *Posthumous Poems of Percy Bysshe Shelley*, with MWS's preface, written because she received nothing from Leigh Hunt (see 18 September 1823). On 17 July the *Literary Gazette, and Journal of Belles Lettres*, finds her preface 'a panegyric' which is 'too hyperbolical to be the effusion of genuine sorrow'.

1	She sees *Charles the Second* and other works by Payne at Covent Garden. This month she also sees several opera productions including *Don Giovanni* and *The Marriage of Figaro*.
8	On a calm night, after a visit to Jane Williams in Kentish Town, she records feeling happier again, certain that she will be reunited with PBS. She feels her 'powers' again (see 14 May) – and will again experience 'the enthusiastic glow of composition' as 'the winged ideas arise' (*Journals*, p. 479).
17	MWS goes with Bessy Kent, other members of Marianne Hunt's family, and Jane Williams, to see Tom Kent in his début as Richard III at Covent Garden.
21	MWS and Percy move to 5 Bartholomew Place, Kentish Town. Jane Williams lives nearby at 12 Mortimer Terrace.

July

She meets the poet 'Arthur Brooke' (John Chalk Claris), a widower who admires PBS's work, several times.

9 (Fri)	She goes to see Byron's body lying in state at 20 Great George Street.
12	She watches Byron's funeral procession go up Highgate Hill.
17	After breakfasting at James Kenney's with Thomas Moore, whom she now begins to help gather materials for his *Letters and Journals of Lord Byron* (1830), she is introduced to Washington Irving, who is a friend of Payne and visiting England this summer.
26	MWS and Jane Williams attend a Novello musical evening. (On 10 October she tells Marianne Hunt that she is at the Novellos' monthly and the Godwins' weekly.)

Percy has recently started school.

August

After the sale of 309 copies, *Posthumous Poems* is withdrawn at the insistence of Sir Timothy Shelley; in order to obtain 'a sufficiency' MWS must agree not to bring PBS's name before the public again during his father's lifetime (Letters, i.444).

Trelawny, still in Greece, sends MWS his account of the 'Cavern Fortress of Mt. Parnassus belonging to General ... Ulysses', asking her to edit it into a form suitable for publication in the *Examiner*. (See Journals, p. 482, n.4.)

Pietro Gamba comes to London and sees much of MWS between now and his return to Greece in March 1825. They reminisce about their life in Pisa and Genoa and he tells her about Byron's last days.

She, Jane Williams, and Louisa Holcroft, who is visiting London, go to hear the soprano Giuditta Pasta as Romeo in Zingarelli's *Giulietta e Romeo* at the King's Theatre. MWS later recalls that 'never did any so move, so penetrate the human heart' as Pasta, by whom 'the tenderest sympathy was awakened, joined to that soft return to one's own past afflictions, which subdued the soul and opened the fountain of tears' (*Rambles*, 1844, in *Novels and Selected Works*, 8.121). They also go to Weber's *Der Freischütz* at the English Opera House several times.

| 10 (Tues) | She goes to the Haymarket to see James Kenney and Isaac Nathan's *The Alcaid* and meets Washington Irving there. |

September

Some time this month or later MWS begins to be invited to gatherings at the house of Dr William Kitchiner. Here she meets, probably for the first time, Diana Mary Dods, who writes as David Lindsay, and Lord Dillon (Seymour, pp. 372–3).

3 (Fri)   Gamba sends MWS a copy of Byron's 'On this day I complete my thirty-sixth year', which she copies into her journal (Journals, pp. 271–3 and n.4).

October

7 (Thurs)   Bryan Waller Procter marries Anne Skepper. This explains why MWS has not seen him for some time. She has, she feels, lost yet another friend.

23   Publication of Medwin's *Conversations of Lord Byron*. MWS objects to the references to PBS's life and to the many inaccuracies.

November

Probably this month she writes to Hogg to ask if he can lend her some Cicero. She is reading him by 3 December.

10 (Wed)   John Cam Hobhouse sends MWS the proofs of his 'Exposure of the Mis-Statements Contained in Captain Medwin's Pretended "Conversations of Lord Byron"' (*Westminster Review*, January 1825). She writes to supply him with further corrections.

December

About now, as a result of a misunderstanding involving an incorrectly delivered message, MWS breaks off her friendship with John Howard Payne until April 1825.

As in August, she is paid £50 by Whitton and wrongly concludes that this is an instalment of an annual £200 from Sir Timothy.

13 (Mon)   *Frank-in-Steam; or, the Modern Promise to Pay* opens at the Olympic Theatre for four nights.

22   Henry Crabb Robinson sees MWS at the Godwins'. She is 'an interesting and charming creature' (*On Books and their Writers*, p. 316).

1825

February

19 (Sat)   She writes to Hobhouse to ask him to arrange for her to watch a debate in the House of Commons; she wants the

parliamentary speeches in *The Last Man* to sound authentic. His favourable reply reaches her probably on 26 (Letters, i.470, n.1).

26   MWS sees Kean as Othello with Jane Williams, Godwin, and Pietro Gamba.

April

8 (Fri)   Recently she has been reading 'my beloved Georgics' and Shaftesbury's *Characteristics* and has seen the Novellos and Horace Smith (Letters, i.476, 477).

8   She has read Leigh Hunt's piece on PBS, much of which is eventually published in his *Lord Byron and Some of his Contemporaries* (1828). Changes she wants include the omission of reference to CC, who has not as yet, fortunately for her reputation, been mentioned by other Byron memoirists.

14   Various misunderstandings having been sorted out, MWS and Payne resume their friendship. On 24 Payne sends her the later volumes of James Fenimore Cooper's *Lionel Lincoln*, which she finds disappointing.

May

4 (Wed)   MWS, while writing in friendly terms to Payne, tries to discourage his love, as in several letters of the next few weeks.

7   MWS and Jane Williams are at the opera with Payne. He supplies tickets for other occasions including a concert at Drury Lane on 21.

30   The Godwins, following the bankruptcy of their book-selling business, move to 44 Gower Place, London.

June

19 (Sun)   MWS entertains Payne and the Godwins. On 23 the same group and William Godwin, Jr, dine at the Godwins'.

25   Payne declares his love and is politely rejected. MWS tells him that she would like to know his friend Irving better, and he interprets this as an invitation to match-making.

26   She sees Novello.

July

This summer, MWS says, she feels happy for the first time since PBS's death (Journals, p. 489 and n.6; Letters, i.500).

7 (Thurs)   She sees Kean in Payne's *Brutus*.

11   She entertains the Lambs, the Godwins, and Payne.

August

In August or September MWS and Jane Williams go to see Caroline
Boaden's comedy *Quite Correct* at the Haymarket. They also spend
ten days at Windsor, one of the settings of *The Last Man*.

Early this month Payne goes to Paris (until July 1826).

16 (Tues)   Without MWS's knowledge, Payne sends Irving his
            letters from her. Earlier in the summer Payne showed
            MWS his letters from Irving.

September

Between 15 (Thurs) and 26 MWS and her stepmother go to Salieri's
            Tarare at the English Opera House (Lyceum). She finds
            the piece dull and some of the music 'tolerable'.

October

14 (Fri)   The Hunts arrive in London after three years in Italy. She
            sees them regularly once more.

November

She reads Moore's life of Sheridan.

Percy is seriously ill with measles but soon recovers.

29 (Tues)   The first part of *The Last Man* goes to press; the last sec-
            tions are ready to go by 1 January 1826.

December

8 (Thurs)   MWS dates her poem 'On reading Wordsworth's Lines
            on Peel Castle' (*Journals*, pp. 494–5).

1826

Presumption is revived this year at the English Opera House.

   John Watson Dalby's laudatory 'Sonnet. Written after Reading
"Valperga," a Tale, by Mary Wollstonecraft Shelley', appears in *The
Pocket Magazine of Classic and Polite Literature*, n.s. 4, p. 360.

January

23 (Mon)   *The Last Man*, by 'the Author of *Frankenstein*', is pub-
            lished in three volumes by Henry Colburn at 27s. MWS
            has received £300 from the publisher. The 'Second

Edition', later this year, is a reprint. Reviews are on the whole unfavourable. The *Monthly Review, or Literary Journal*, n.s. 1, for March, p. 334, considers *The Last Man* to be 'The offspring of a diseased imagination, and of a most polluted taste'; the *Ladies' Monthly Museum* 23, also for March, p. 169, comments 'We should be better pleased to see [MWS] exercise her powers of intellect on subjects less removed from nature and probability'. Mention of her name by reviewers causes Sir Timothy Shelley to 'withhold funds'.

Soon after 23 MWS writes the short poem 'To Jane – (with the "Last Man")' (Journals, p. 495).

February
25 (Sat)   She tells John Bowring that she believes PBS was regulated by different laws to those governing 'us common mortals'; she has tried to give some idea of him in Adrian in *The Last Man* (Letters, i.512).

March
c. 20 (Mon) Publication in Paris of an unauthorized Galignani edition of *The Last Man*.

April
4 (Tues)   Henry Colburn buys unsold copies of the second edition of *Frankenstein* in order to reissue them.
4   MWS asks Bowring to recommend or lend some Spanish books.
6   Godwin tells his wife, who has complained of his closeness to MWS, that he sees her about twice a week.
c. 18   MWS and Jane Williams watch a show by the comic actor Charles Mathews.

She continues to take great interest in the affairs of Greece, as she tells Payne in a letter of 21 after the fall of Missolonghi.

May
This month or in early June MWS and Jane Williams enjoy pretending to be Italians, which makes their lack of a chaperon less surprising, at a performance of works including act one of Meyerbeer's *Il*

crociato in Egitto. They also attend Pasta's benefit night (Johann Simon Mayr's *Medea*).

June

10 (Sat)   *Le Monstre et le magicien*, based on *Frankenstein*, by Jean Toussaint Merle and Antoine Nicolas Béread, opens at the Théâtre Porte Saint-Martin, Paris, and runs for an unusual ninety-four performances. Thomas Potter Cooke repeats his monster (see August 1823). MWS hopes to read a printed version of the piece (Letters, iii.403).

11   MWS's letter in defence of the castrato Giovanni-Battista Velluti, signed 'Anglo-Italicus', is published in *The Examiner*. She wrote it on 29 May. She sends a continuation on 23 but it is not published.

18   MWS and Williams are at Velluti's benefit night.

July

3 (Mon)   Henry M. Milner's *The Man and the Monster; or, the Fate of Frankenstein* opens at the Royal Coburg and lasts eight performances.

4–9   British newspaper articles on the alleged reanimation of a seventeenth-century Englishman, Roger Dodsworth, begin to appear following the original item in *Le Journal du commerce de Lyon* on 28 June (*Collected Tales*, p. 377); see September.

13   MWS is at the Hunts' with the journalist Peter George Patmore, Henry Crabb Robinson, and the Lambs.

By 28   Payne has arrived in London after nearly a year in Paris. On 29 a messenger delivers to her some books she has asked him to obtain in Paris – two copies of the Galignani *Works of Lord Byron* and possibly a copy of *Le Monstre et le magicien*. He probably sees MWS on 30 (Letters, iii.404).

August

Between about 5 (Sat) of this month and 2 September MWS and Jane Williams are in Brighton and the Sussex village of Sompting. To MWS this is a month of happiness with her dearest friend, yet Williams thanks God it is over. Back in Kentish Town MWS feels desolate and unloved but recovers her serenity within a few days (Journals, pp. 497–9).

12   After this date she starts work on 'A Visit to Brighton'
            and her review of books about Italy (see Letters i.527,
            October, and December).

September
7 (Thurs) Amelia Curran's portrait of PBS reaches MWS after
            much delay.
14   The death of Charles Shelley makes Percy Florence
            Shelley heir to the baronetcy.

By about September or October MWS has written 'Roger Dodsworth:
the Reanimated Englishman' and sends it to the *New Monthly
Magazine*. It remains unpublished until 1863.

October
MWS's review of books about Italy by Charlotte Ann Eaton, Anna
Brownell Jameson, and the Marquess of Normanby is published in
the *Westminster Review*, vol. 6, pp. 325–41.
She sends work by Diana Mary Dods ('David Lindsay'), by now a
close friend, to publishers.
9 (Mon)   John Kerr's *The Monster and the Magician; or, the Fate of
            Frankenstein* (translated from the French version – see 10
            June), opens for about four performances at the New
            Royal West London Theatre.
30   MWS offers *Proserpine* and *Midas* to the editor of the
            Literary Souvenir, Alaric Watts (Letters i.532).
30   She writes to tell Hunt that she will, when possible,
            honour PBS's intention of leaving him £2000.

December
MWS's essay 'A Visit to Brighton' is in the *London Magazine*, vol. 16,
pp. 460–6.
She may also be the author of 'Lacy de Vere', published late this year
in *Forget-Me-Not for 1827*, pp. 275–94.

1827

January
By *c.* 11 (Thurs) MWS has decided on Perkin Warbeck as the subject
            of her next novel (Letters, i.538).

February

She writes a sonnet in Spanish and, on 14 (Wed), copies it into her Journal. She shows it to Moore in early July; it suggests to him the words for his 'Hope comes again, – to this heart long a stranger'.

April

At some point between now and July Jane Williams becomes Hogg's common-law wife. MWS, who does not much like Hogg and feels that she is losing her dearest friend – see also 13 July – tries to seem happy about this development.

2 (Mon)   Lord Dillon calls.

May

Sir Timothy Shelley agrees to meet his grandson, Percy, for the first time.

June

21 (Thurs) and 25 MWS sees Moore and gives him extensive information for his work on Byron. She is surprised to find that she can talk to Moore with great freedom; he seems to understand her and to like her (*Journals*, p. 501).

July

1 (Sun), 4, and 8 She sees Moore again and continues to supply information, written and spoken, for his book. She writes down for him what she can remember of Byron's burnt memoirs and even confides to him the details of his relationship with CC. After he leaves London on 11 she continues to write to him regularly and to play an important role in shaping parts of his work on Byron.

3   She condoles with Guiccioli on the death of her brother Pietro Gamba in Greece, as again more extensively in a letter of 20 August.

13   'My friend has proved false & treacherous!' (*Journals*, p. 502). Isabel Robinson (see 24 July) has relayed to MWS some of the gossip Jane Williams Hogg has been spreading about her and her inadequacy as PBS's wife. MWS delays confronting her friend, who is ill with a difficult pregnancy and then convalescing.

19   She dines at the Godwins with Payne.

23   CC sends MWS money to help her cope with her poverty as she awaits the finalizing of a new settlement with Sir Timothy Shelley. MWS also borrows from Hogg (£7 in May, £10 in August).

24   She vacates her Kentish Town lodgings and travels to Worthing in Sussex with Percy, the Hunts' daughter Mary, Isabel Robinson and her baby Adeline. MWS has known Robinson for some months and is helping her conceal from her family and society at large that she is an unmarried mother. She is known as Mrs Douglas, and it is planned that she will soon go to France with Diana Mary Dods, who will be disguised as her 'husband' Mr Walter Sholto Douglas. In correspondence this summer and autumn MWS aids the deception by mentioning Isabel's forthcoming marriage.

29   MWS and her group move into lodgings in the village of Sompting, Sussex. Here she reads some Greek, works on *Perkin Warbeck* and materials for Moore, enjoys country walks, and nurses the often ill Isabel Robinson/Douglas.

August

8 (Wed)   Death of George Canning, briefly prime minister and formerly foreign secretary. MWS feels that although his liberalism at home may survive, his unrivalled experience and 'tact' in foreign policy is a loss to other countries as well as his own (Letters, i.559–60).

26   The Sompting accommodation is to be re-let to tenants who can pay more. MWS and Isabel Douglas find cheaper lodgings a few miles away in Arundel on 27. While they wait for these to become available they take rooms at the inn in Sompting from 29.

30   MWS's thirtieth birthday.

September

1 (Sat)   After much negotiation with, and delay from, Sir Timothy, annual payments to MWS of £250 are authorized. He will also help finance Percy's education but stipulates that MWS must continue to live in England. As soon as she actually receives some of the money on 7 she repays Hogg's recent loan of £10.

3	MWS's group moves to Mrs Cooper's, Tarrant Street, Arundel.
17	She tells Jane Hogg that she is doing some writing in the mornings. She is evidently working on *Perkin Warbeck*, since Godwin is sending her related historical material by late September, as he continues to do throughout the period of the novel's composition.
23	Dods, probably now in the guise of Walter Sholto Douglas, arrives in Arundel. MWS at once writes to Payne to ask if he can obtain a passport for the group (including, at this stage, herself and Percy, but not Mary Hunt, who goes home to London by 13 October). Since 'Mr and Mrs Douglas' are unable to be present in person, she sends him samples of their signatures. With the aid of forged signatures and, probably, actors impersonating members of the group, Payne succeeds in obtaining the passports and sending them by 1 October. (See *Letters*, ii.12, n.2.)
25	MWS again, as on 30 October last year, offers *Proserpine* and *Midas* to the *Literary Souvenir*.
26	She has, she feels (*Journals*, p. 503), 'shaken off the dead calm of my life – interesting myself deeply for one whose destiny is so strange' (Isabel Douglas).

October

Some time between 9 (Tues) and 13 the social reformer Fanny Wright, who has lived in America since 1818, visits MWS in Arundel. She tries unsuccessfully to persuade her to go back with her to her Nashoba community in Tennessee.

MWS intends to go to Dieppe for a month with the Douglases. She does not, partly because Percy has been ill. The Douglases depart on or after 13.

By 26 MWS and Percy have returned to London. On 27 they go to stay with Fanny Wright in Harrow, where she meets Wright's friends the Trollopes.

31	MWS, Wright, and the reformers Robert Owen and his son Robert Dale Owen visit Godwin.

November

They move into 51 George Street, Portman Square, London. Probably soon afterwards, she asks Payne for tickets to see Kean at Covent Garden ('Newly Uncovered Letters and Poems', p. 57; not at Drury Lane as Bennett states p. 56, n. 20), where his roles this autumn are Shylock, Richard III, and Sir Giles Overreach.

4 (Sun)   MWS sees off Fanny Wright and Fanny Trollope, who is accompanying her to America with three of her children on the *Edward*.

MWS may be the author of 'The Convent of Chaillot; or, Vallière and Louis XIV', in *The Keepsake for MDCCCXXVIII*. She also publishes there three 'Fragments' by PBS, including 'The Aziola'.

December

5 (Wed)   She feels alone and inconsolable in London with one friend, Jane Williams Hogg, lost, and another, Isabel Douglas, absent (Journals, p. 505). Edward Coote Pinkney's satire *The New Frankenstein* appears in *The Marylander*.

This winter she continues to make good use of theatre tickets supplied by Payne.

1828

January

23 (Wed)   She sees Godwin, Payne, and the actor Thomas Abthorpe Cooper, Godwin's relation and former ward, who is visiting from America.

February

9 (Sat)   Moore calls on MWS. On 11, on his advice, she confronts Jane Williams Hogg over the defamation which she has known about, and been angry or wounded about, since July 1827. Three days later she makes her feelings of loss and betrayal clearer by letter. The friendship, if damaged, survives.

12	She lists among the few people she sees Lord Dillon, Georgiana 'Gee' Paul (daughter of MWS's Pisa acquaintance Emily Beauclerk and her husband Charles, and wife of John Dean Paul), and the Robinsons – Isabel's family, whom she has known since February 1827 or earlier.
19	Moore has persuaded John Murray to send MWS £100, which she likes to think is an advance on *Perkin Warbeck*. (See 12 November 1829.) She also thanks Murray for sending the works of John Ford, which she no doubt wants for his *Perkin Warbeck* in particular.
20	Moore calls.

In late February and early March MWS asks John Bowring several times to lend her his Byron letters so that she can copy them for Moore. She has obtained at least some of them by 10 April. (See 'Newly Uncovered Letters and Poems', pp. 57–60.)

March
7 (Fri)	She sees Isabel Baxter Booth.
11	In response to rumours about her relationship with Vincent Novello she regretfully ends their friendship, enclosing in her letter a lock of her mother's hair.
25	Percy begins boarding at Edward Slater's Gentlemen's Academy, Kensington, where the fees are £45 a year. On 14, as again in June, September, and December, she writes to Whitton to ask him to inform Sir Timothy Shelley how difficult her financial circumstances now are.

April
11 (Fri)	MWS sets out for Paris with Julia Robinson, Isabel's younger sister. Soon after arrival at the Douglases' lodgings MWS falls ill with smallpox. She is convalescent by 23 and out of bed on 27. Her face is marked only temporarily by the disease.

May
After her recovery she meets, through the Garnett family (friends of Wright and the Douglases) French writers including Prosper Mérimée, Benjamin Constant, Claude Fauriel, and the revolutionary hero General Lafayette. Her relationship with Mérimée is particularly

close: Harriet Garnett, whom she first meets on 11 (Sun), mentions her flirting with him at her farewell gathering on 24 (Letters ii.34, n. 3, 40 n.2), and the same evening she returns a letter from him (no longer extant) because, she says, she is not a coquette and he may come to regret the sentiments he has expressed (Letters, ii.40).

26   MWS and Julia Robinson leave Paris. She remains on the coast, first at Dover, because she does not want to show her disfigurement in London and doctors have recommended sea-bathing.

June

By 5 (Thurs) they are living at Mrs Dawson's, Snargate Street, Over the Sluice, Dover. An unspecified financial difficulty keeps her in Dover – she intends to move to Hastings – longer than intended.

9–13   *Presumption* is performed at the Theatre Royal, Liverpool.

11   MWS suggests to John Bowring of the *Westminster Review* that she should review a recent work by Prosper Mérimée; see January 1829.

17   Joshua Robinson, father of Isabel and Julia, brings Percy to join his mother and stays until 23. (Percy stays until the end of his holidays in late July.)

20   MWS strongly recommends Manzoni's recently published *I promessi sposi* to Jane Williams Hogg.

23   MWS, Julia Robinson, and Percy move to Hastings. Godwin joins them on 25 and leaves on 30. Joshua Robinson visits on 30.

August

7 (Thurs)   She arrives at Park Cottage, Paddington, to stay with the Robinsons (until December). Julia Robinson is seriously ill.

9   She calls on her father. As she is still marked by smallpox and has cropped hair, however, she goes out very rarely.

15 and 16   She asks John Bowring for histories of Spain in connection with research for *Perkin Warbeck*. Later in the month she requests similar material from Murray.

September

She approaches Mérimée about French sources for *Perkin*.
She has now recovered sufficiently to start going to the theatre regularly, provided with tickets by Payne as usual.

October

Still reading widely for the novel, she asks Ollier for historical material on 14. Later in the month she writes to Thomas Crofton Croker, author of *Researches in the South of Ireland*, for Irish sources. Croker later reads the Irish chapters for her.

16 (Thurs)   CC arrives in England. MWS sees her at the Godwins'. Charles Clairmont and his wife and daughters have also been in London since July.

30   MWS probably sees Kean as Othello at Covent Garden (Letters, ii.64).

November

This month she translates ballads by Mérimée. (See Letters, ii.62, n.2.) Her stories 'The Sisters of Albano' and 'Ferdinando Eboli: a Tale' are published in *The Keepsake for MDCCCXXIX* as the work of 'the Author of *Frankenstein*'.

1 (Sat)   Thomas Crofton Croker probably visits MWS.

15   She sees Trelawny for the first time since 1823. He seems to like her less than he used to; she feels he can no longer confide in her and wilfully misunderstands her (Letters, ii.82). He goes abroad again in January 1829.

By about 17 she has read James Boaden's *The Man of Two Lives*.

28   She drives with Moore.

December

24 (Wed)   MWS, CC and Percy move to 4 Oxford Terrace, London.

1829

January

MWS's review of recent works by Prosper Mérimée appears in the *Westminster Review*, vol. 10, pp. 71–81. One of these works, *La Guzla*, is an influence on MWS's 'The Evil Eye'. (See *Collected Tales and Stories*, p. 379, and November.)

February

4 (Wed)   She writes to Mérimée about her plans for a life either of the Empress Josephine or of Mme de Staël. Later in the year she proposes the idea to Murray without success.

21   She calls on Moore.

28   She is probably at Farquhar's *The Beaux' Stratagem* at
            Covent Garden. This year she is again frequently at the
            theatre and begins taking Percy with her to at least some
            productions.

March
18 (Wed)   Lord Dillon, writing to MWS, contrasts her quiet femi-
            nine manner with his expectation – based on her work –
            that she would be enthusiastic, extravagant.

April
MWS refuses to supply Trelawny with biographical materials on
PBS. She wants to avoid public notoriety for herself and for PBS; one
day she intends to write his life herself, but now is not the time
(Letters, ii.72).

By 5 (Sun) CC has moved to live with her brother Charles and his
            family at 5 Carmarthen Street. (Later this year Charles
            has to borrow money from MWS to enable him to return
            to Vienna after various schemes for employment in
            London founder. See July 1845.)
By 6 MWS is staying again with the Robinsons at Park Cottage.
9   She probably goes to Rossini's *La gazza ladra* at the
            King's Theatre with Payne and members of the Robinson
            family (Letters, ii. 73–4).

This spring she begins helping Cyrus Redding with PBS material
for the Galignani edition of *The Poetical Works of Coleridge, Shelley
and Keats*.

May
13 (Wed)   MWS moves to 33 Somerset Street, Portman Square,
            London.
20 and 22   She sees Moore.
25   She writes to Sir Walter Scott to ask if he can suggest any
            material on Warbeck in Scotland less familiar than the
            histories she has already consulted.

June
1 (Mon)   Sir Timothy Shelley increases MWS's annuity from
            £250 to £300.

Some time between 4 of this month and 1 July she is at the Royal
Academy exhibition.
5   Moore visits.

July
MWS's review of accounts of Italy by Henry Digby Beste and Louis
Simond is published in the *Westminster Review*, vol. 11, pp. 127–40.
She sent Bowring the proofs on 1 June.
c. 6 (Mon) She asks Ollier to lend her Edward Bulwer's *Devereux*.

August
12 (Wed)   Moore breakfasts with MWS.
19   She is with Amelia Curran at the Godwins', as again on 4
              September.
29   She suggests to John Bowring that she should review
              Anna Brownell Jameson's *The Loves of the Poets* for the
              Westminster Review.

September
Possibly on 3 (Thurs) – see Letters, ii.86 – MWS tells Cyrus Redding
              that she is tempted to write a brief life of PBS for the
              Galignani edition if her authorship can be kept secret. In
              the event Redding writes it. At some point between now
              and November she tells him that the tone of his memoir
              sounds wrong but he has included no great untruths
              (Letters, ii.87).
12   Godwin and Amelia Curran visit MWS.
18   CC leaves London to return to Dresden.
30   Moore visits MWS.

October
Her review of Jameson's *The Loves of the Poets* is published in *The
Westminster Review*, vol. 11, pp. 472–7.
7 (Wed) or 8 She is at Sir Thomas Lawrence's while Moore sits for
              his portrait. Later she goes with Moore to Charterhouse
              school to see his son.

November
4 (Thurs)   By this date she has completed the final version of the
              first volume of *Perkin Warbeck* and is revising and cutting
              her material for the second and third.

c. 9–10 She hears from Moore that Murray has refused *Perkin*. She hopes that she can produce something else for the £100 Murray sent her in February 1828; she feels strongly that she is not owed anything for helping Moore because she has vowed not to make money from her association with Byron. On 12 Murray sends a receipt for £100 'value received'.

11 MWS's story 'The False Rhyme' is published in the *Athenaeum*. (See also the end of this month.)

13 She offers *Perkin* to Henry Colburn; she is frustrated to receive no reply until January 1830.

This month MWS's stories 'The Mourner', 'The Evil Eye', and 'The False Rhyme' are published in *The Keepsake for MDCCCXXX* as the work of 'the Author of *Frankenstein*'. 'Ritratto di Ugo Foscolo' (translated from Foscolo's 'Sonetto autoritratto'), signed 'M.S.' in *The Bijou for 1830*, may also be hers; see *Novels and Selected Works*, i.238.)

December

7 (Tues) She asks Murray for a copy of Irving's *The Conquest of Granada* and has received it by *c.* 13. On 7 January 1830 she proposes reviewing it for the *Westminster Review*.

c. 15 Publication in Paris of the Galignani *Poetical Works of Coleridge, Shelley and Keats*.

22 She has read Stendhal's *Promenades dans Rome*, probably in order to review it for the *Foreign Quarterly Review* or perhaps intending to translate it, but finds it impossibly dull and commonplace (Letters, ii.97 and n.1).

1830

MWS's 'The False Rhyme' is reprinted in *The Polar Star of Entertainment and Popular Science, and Universal Repertorium of General Literature*, vol. 2, pp. 171–2.

January

5 (Wed) MWS accepts, through Ollier, Colburn's somewhat disappointing offer to buy the copyright of *Perkin Warbeck* for £150. She signs the agreement with Colburn and Bentley, publishers, on 21.

7	MWS is deeply affected by the death of Sir Thomas Lawrence so soon after she saw him with Moore.
18	Publication by Murray of the first volume of Moore's *Letters and Journals of Lord Byron*. MWS, who has herself given Moore considerable assistance, on 19 praises Moore's 'elegant and forcible' style and is pleased to meet again 'our Lord Byron – the fascinating – faulty – childish – philosophical being' and the reconcilingly 'delightful and buoyant tone of his conversation and manners' (to Murray, Letters, ii.101–2).
22	'I have begun a new kind of life somewhat – going a little into society – & forming a variety of acquaintances'; although people take her up and then leave her alone and her poverty is a barrier, she is 'often amused and sometimes interested' (Journals, pp. 512–13).

February

5 (Sat)　William Godwin, Jr, marries Emily Eldred.

March

Early this month MWS sends Colburn and Bentley the manuscript of most of *Perkin*. On 5 (Fri), at last, they express the intention of publishing it as soon as possible; she expects to be busy with it over the next two or three weeks (Letters, ii.106). She is also continuing to investigate the possibility of writing a life of Germaine de Staël or the Empress Josephine.

At some time between early March and mid-April she writes a review of her father's novel *Cloudesley* (see May).

25	She gives a party at which the guests include Croker, Bulwer, Godwin, Julia Robinson, Moore, Irving, Kenney, the writer Lady Mary Shepherd, the geologist Roderick Impey Murchison, the lawyer and essayist Charles Jerningham, Ellen Manners-Sutton, wife of the Speaker of the House of Commons and sister of Lady Blessington, and Gee Paul with her husband John, her father-in-law Sir John, and her sister-in-law Anne-Frances Hare and family.

April

6 (Tues)	MWS, Godwin, Sir John Paul, and Ellen Manners-Sutton attend an evening party at the Hares'.

10   MWS and Moore are among the guests at the Manners-
            Suttons'.
19   The printers temporarily mislay the first 44 pages of the
            third volume of *Perkin*.
29   She meets Godwin to discuss the publishers' suggestion
            that the novel's title should be changed because another
            novel, Alexander Campbell's *Perkin Warbeck; or, the Court
            of James the Fourth of Scotland* is about to appear. She per-
            suades Colburn and Bentley to keep her original title.

May

MWS's review of Godwin's *Cloudesley* is in *Blackwood's Edinburgh
Magazine*, vol. 27, pp. 711–16. Her 'The False Rhyme' is reprinted in
The Casket, Flowers of Literature, Wit & Sentiment, no. 5, pp. 203–4.

13 (Thurs) *The Fortunes of Perkin Warbeck, A Romance* is published in
            three volumes by Colburn and Bentley. Among the
            reviews the *Athenaeum* for 29 of this month objects in
            general to historical romances but believes that this one
            displays 'a noble energy of thought – a deep concentra-
            tion of feeling', and the *New Monthly Magazine and
            Literary Journal* for November says that it is 'written with
            great energy, both of thought and expression', as well as
            with 'feminine delicacy of thought and feeling'. The
            Edinburgh Literary Journal for 12 June, however, feels that
            truth and fiction are not blended with sufficient skill.
29   MWS, Godwin, and Julia and Rosa Robinson attend an
            exhibition of paintings by Sir Thomas Lawrence at the
            British Gallery.

June

7 (Mon)   MWS entertains Ellen Manners-Sutton, Jerningham,
            Godwin, Moore, Bulwer, the Irish artist Richard
            Rothwell, members of the Robinson family, and others.
18   The poet and essayist Maria Jane Jewsbury, who met
            MWS through Rothwell on 16 or 17, describes her
            impression of MWS to Anna Jameson: her 'union of
            buoyancy and depth', kind manners and 'habit of amica-
            ble feeling', and natural hilarity contrast puzzlingly with
            'the almost sadly profound nature of some of her
            remarks'. She seems neither a happy woman nor 'one

	that could be distinctly termed melancholy' (*Anna Jameson: Letters and Friendships*, ed. Mrs Steuart Erskine (1915), pp. 89–90).
26	Death of King George IV; succeeded by William IV.

July

She spends most of the month in Southend, setting off probably on 30 June. She and Percy come back to London for a ball at the Manners-Suttons', probably on 16 (Fri) or 17. They are also in London on 24–25.

August

5 (Thurs)	She begins a three-month stay with the Robinsons at Park Cottage, Paddington.
9	She is still hoping to write a life of Mme de Staël for Murray's Family Library series. Failing that, she suggests other possibilities to him: a life of the Prophet Mohammed, an account of the conquest of Mexico and Peru, a history of English manners and literature in the eighteenth century, or lives of the English philosophers.

This month she sees much of Anne-Frances Hare.

September

8 (Wed)	Having received no answer to her letter of 9 August she writes with further ideas, in Murray's absence, to his son John Murray III: an account of prehistory, the lives of famous women, a history of woman and society, or a history of chivalry. She also suggests that she could write for the *Quarterly Review*.
18	Death of Hazlitt.
24	The Hares are about to depart for Italy. MWS remembers agreeable evenings spent with them and with the Pauls; her 'intimacy' with Gee Paul has begun (*Journals*, p. 515). On one occasion Gabriele Rossetti (Italian patriot, poet, and father of subsequently famous children) was there too and performed improvizations.

October

Publication of MWS's review of Mérimée's *1572. Chronique du temps de Charles IX* in the *Westminster Review*, vol. 13, pp. 495–502.

November
MWS's stories 'Transformation' and 'The Swiss Peasant', by 'the Author of *Frankenstein*', and her poems 'Absence', 'A Dirge', and 'A Night Scene' are published in *The Keepsake for MDCCCXXXI*.

4 (Thurs)   She moves back to 33 Somerset Street.

11   She writes to congratulate Lafayette on the July Revolution in France. In England there is hope that the new king will help the cause of reform, but in the meantime the people suffer crippling levels of taxation.

December
1 (Wed)   She feels alone, disappointed, and depressed. She saw Isabel Douglas on 30 November and wonders how she could ever have adored her (Journals, pp. 516–17; Bennett in 'Newly Uncovered Letters and Poems', p. 64, corrects the identification from Isabel Baxter Booth – Journals, p. 516, n. 7 – to Isabel Douglas.)

17   Moore calls on MWS.

On 18 she writes about her loneliness, her poverty, and her despair of ever finding reciprocal love (Journals, p. 517). By 27 she has read the manuscript of Trelawny's recollections. She finds much to admire, but counsels the omission of passages of out-of-date and objectionable 'coarseness'. She will need to edit the work if it is to be published.

Towards the end of this month or early the next the second volume of Moore's Byron appears.

30   She offers *Midas* for inclusion in Rudolph Ackermann's juvenile library series (Letters, ii.122).

1831

'Transformation', by 'the Author of *Frankenstein*', is published by E. Littell of Philadelphia in *The Spirit of the Annuals, for MDCCCXXXI*.

January
Early in the year MWS begins planning her novel *Lodore*.

11 (Tues)   She has been reading Bulwer's *Paul Clifford* and finds it 'sublime' (Journals, p. 517).

30   She is at the Murchisons' with guests including John
            Gibson Lockhart, editor of the *Quarterly Review*, the nov-
            elist and journalist Theodore Hook, and Murray.

Writing to Ollier probably this month or next she suggests that she
could write a weekly article for the *Court Journal*. She sends him,
probably in February, an unidentified 'paper' intended for this or
the *New Monthly Magazine* (Letters ii.126, 129).

February
5 (Sat)   She goes to Rossini's *Il barbiere di Siviglia* at the King's
            Theatre and meets John Paul, his father, and Lincoln
            Stanhope, son of the Earl of Harrington.
13   MWS goes to the Temple Church with John and Gee
            Paul to hear Rev. Christopher Benson preach.
14   She is at the King's Theatre again to hear Giovanni
            Davide in Rossini. On 17 she hears him in Cimarosa's *Il
            matrimonio segreto*.
18   She is working on a brief memoir of her father (see
            1 April), probably completed by the end of the month.
            She asks Ollier whether Colburn and Bentley might
            publish a new edition of *Frankenstein* in the same series
            as their one-volume *Caleb Williams*. By 10 March this
            has become at least a possibility (Letters, ii.129).

March
Journal entries continue to suggest frequent mood swings.
2 (Sun)   MWS is at the house of Mary Wood, daughter of the
            prime minister, Earl Grey, and her husband Charles.
            Other guests include Godwin, Payne, Leicester Stanhope
            – with Byron at Missolonghi, brother of Lincoln
            Stanhope – and possibly the poet Thomas Campbell
            (Letters, ii.127, n.1).
5   MWS goes to Rossini's *La Cenerentola* at the King's Theatre.
16   She acknowledges receipt of £5 5s. from Colburn and
            Bentley for the memoir of Godwin.
21   She sends an unidentified article to William Blackwood
            of *Blackwood's Magazine*. Presumably it is rejected.
22–25   She writes at length to Trelawny about the difficulties
            she is experiencing in arranging the publication of his

recollections by Colburn and Bentley. She also includes the first of a series of references in their correspondence over the next few months to the idea that she and Trelawny should marry. The remarks are, at least at first, intended to remain jocular; see, however, 26 July. Trelawny may actually propose marriage at some point before then (see Letters, ii.140–1 and n.1).

April

1 (Fri)   MWS's 'Memoir of William Godwin' is published with the Colburn and Bentley edition of his *Caleb Williams*.

10   She dines at Emily Beauclerk's with her daughter Gee Paul, son Major Aubrey Beauclerk, and other family members.

29   MWS is part of a large party who are at the house of Lady Paul, Gee's mother-in-law, to see *tableaux vivants*.

May

Early in the month MWS is ill and 'cast down'.

10 (Tues)   She asks Ollier to send her Catherine Frances Gore's *The Tuileries* and Benjamin Disraeli's *The Young Duke* – recent novels published by Colburn and Bentley.

18   Rothwell is painting her portrait.

June

She and Julia Robinson go to the Royal Ascot races.

9   (Thurs) Moore visits MWS.

22   She seeks an increase in the amount of money disbursed by Sir Timothy for Percy on the grounds that the next stage of his education, which at this time is expected to be with a private tutor, will entail considerable extra expense. Sir Timothy agrees to the increase by October.

25   She probably attends a party at the Manners-Suttons'.

30   Terms are agreed for publication of the revised *Frankenstein*. She sells Colburn and Bentley the copyright.

July

18 (Mon)   MWS goes to a concert given by Nicolò Paganini at the King's Theatre.

26   She insists that she can never be Trelawny's wife because she expects complete devotion and protection from a husband whereas he belongs to womankind in general.

August

7 (Sun)   She is visited by John Paul and visits the Manners-Suttons and Gee Paul, with whom she sees and dislikes, but is amused by, Sir Francis Vincent. It may be that he is either having an affair with Gee or is sufficiently intimate to give that scandalous impression (Journals, p. 524, n.2; Seymour, p. 421).

14   MWS writes stanzas beginning 'Alas I weep my life away ...' in her journal.

September

8 (Thurs)   She sits in the Earl Marshal's box at the coronation of William IV. Journals, p. 523, n.3, suggests that she is invited because of her friendship with the Beauclerks.

21   Second Reform Bill passed in the House of Commons only to be rejected by the House of Lords on 22.

October

She is spending time with the Pauls and with Gee's sister Jane FitzRoy and her husband Henry FitzRoy.

14 (Fri)   Moore visits MWS.

15   She dates the introduction to the revised *Frankenstein*. The introduction, in which she gives her account of the genesis of the novel, first appears separately on 22 in the *Court Journal*, which is owned by Colburn and Bentley.

31   Publication at 6s. of MWS's revised *Frankenstein* in Colburn and Bentley's Standard Novels. MWS's name appears on the engraved title-page. The first part of a translation from Schiller, *The Ghost-Seer*, is included in the same volume. 4020 copies are printed; of these 3170 copies are sold and 107 given away by 31 August 1832 (*Frankenstein Notebooks*, p. civ). This edition will be reprinted in 1832, 1839, and 1849. The *London Literary Gazette*, reviewing the novel on 19 November, opines that it is 'certainly one of the most original works that ever proceeded from a female pen'; it 'appeals to fear, not love, and ... has less of the heart in it than of the mind'. The new edition also prompts Medwin to print PBS's unpublished review of the first edition (see January

1818) as 'On "Frankenstein"' in the *Athenaeum* for 10 November 1832.

November

'The Dream', by 'the Author of *Frankenstein*', appears in *The Keepsake for MDCCCXXXII* and *Proserpine* in *The Winter's Wreath for MDCC-CXXXII*. This is a revised version of *Proserpine*, no doubt in part because of restrictions on length but also designed to 'turn it into a more adult narrative that places more blame on the parent Ceres than on the child Proserpine' (Charles E. Robinson, ed., *The Mythological Dramas*, pp. 13–14).

18 (Fri)   Gee Paul, guilty or suspected of adultery, has been cast off by her husband and deprived of her child. During the next few months MWS lends her as much support as possible, as do Gee's parents-in-law.

December

She reads the novel *Romance and Reality*, by Letitia Elizabeth Landon ('L.E.L.').

Publication by Colburn and Bentley of Trelawny's *Adventures of a Younger Son*.

1832

Payne returns to America.

January

MWS's review of James Fenimore Cooper's *The Bravo* in the *Westminster Review*, vol. 16, pp. 180–92.

February

She writes, or continues writing, a (lost) review of Bulwer's *Eugene Aram* which is declined by the *Westminster Review*.

Sir Timothy Shelley agrees to increase her allowance to £400 from 1 March. Percy also receives an increase of £50.

6 (Mon)   She witnesses the act of separation between Gee and John Paul. Now reunited with her child, Gee goes to her grandfather's house in Ireland. (She is reconciled to her husband in about 1843 – see *Journals*, p. 524, n.3.)

March

4 (Mon)   MWS calls on John Gregson, her father-in-law's representative, in connection with the increase. As often before, she has difficulty extracting her quarterly payment over the following fortnight.

24   CC, now living in Pisa, asks MWS to edit and complete her story 'The Pole'.

30   MWS, Godwin, and Gabriele Rossetti are at the Stanhopes'.

April

1 (Sun)   Moore calls on MWS.

She sees the Manners-Suttons.

May

At some point after 4 (Fri) she begins writing notes for Moore's *The Works of Lord Byron: with his Letters and Journals* (1832–5).

4   She encourages Murray (unsuccessfully) to publish Godwin's proposed *Lives of the Necromancers* (1834).

14   MWS offers *Midas* for publication in the *Literary Souvenir* or the *New Year's Gift and Juvenile Souvenir*. It will remain unpublished until 1922.

June

4 (Mon)   Third Reform Bill passed.

By *c*. 10 MWS has read Disraeli's *Contarini Fleming*.

15   She and Percy go to Sandgate in Kent for the rest of the summer, partly in order to avoid the cholera epidemic which has reached London.

July

5 (Fri) – 7   She sends 'Angeline', the story revised as 'The Brother and the Sister' (see November) to Frederic Mansel Reynolds, editor of *The Keepsake*.

9   Having edited 'The Pole' and provided it with an ending, she sends it to the *Court Magazine and Belle Assemblée*.

26   She sends her story 'The Invisible Girl' to Reynolds.

August

The first part of CC's 'The Pole' is published, as the work of 'the Author of *Frankenstein*', in the *Court Magazine and Belle Assemblée*. The second part appears in the September issue.

1 (Tues)   Probable date of the arrival at Sandgate of Trelawny and his eighteen-year-old daughter Julia, who is to stay with MWS for a month before leaving for Italy. She finds Julia superficial and her father more difficult: strange, wonderful, but destroyed by his 'envy, & internal dissatisfaction' (Journals, pp. 526–7). His politics remain more radical than hers. He leaves in the last week of the month.

6   MWS learns of the death of Lord Dillon on 24 July.

By 24 Percy has gone back for a few last weeks at his school in Kensington before going to Harrow.

30   MWS's thirty-fifth birthday.

September

8 (Fri)   Death from cholera of William Godwin, Jr, MWS's twenty-nine-year-old half-brother.

c. 15   She escorts Julia Trelawny to Dover.

By 26 MWS and Percy have returned to London.

29   Percy starts at Harrow school.

October

c. 1 (Sun)   MWS goes to stay with Lady Paul, who has a cottage at Harrow, and satisfies herself that Percy is happy at school. She returns to Somerset Street on 8.

25   She asks Ollier for some new reading, suggesting James Morier's *Zohrab the Hostage* or the memoirs of the duchesse d'Abrantès. Ollier, who worked for Colburn from 1823 and Colburn and Bentley from 1829, is now with Bentley, where he remains a useful contact for MWS and her father (Letters, ii.175, n.2).

This autumn she visits the Robinsons several times at their new home in Thames Ditton. She continues work on *Lodore* and reads twelve books of *The Iliad*.

November

This month Henry Crabb Robinson reads *Frankenstein* for the first time, presumably in the 1831 edition, and concludes that it is 'a very powerfully written book, but in the main disgusting. It is very much in Godwin's style, but somewhat softened. The great fault is that Mrs Shelley has not been able to have the show of probability ... It is ridiculous to imagine such incidents in our age. ... The next fault is that the Monster is too benevolent for a Monster' (*On Books and their Writers*, pp. 418–19.)

The Keepsake for MDCCCXXXIII includes her 'Stanzas' beginning 'I must forget thy dark eyes' love-fraught gaze' and 'To love in solitude and mystery' and her stories (as 'the Author of *Frankenstein*') 'The Brother and Sister: an Italian Story' and 'The Invisible Girl'. Both these stories are also published by Carey and Hart of Philadelphia in *Match-Making, and Other Tales*. A translation, 'Le Frère et la soeur', by 'Mistress Shelley', is published in Paris in *Le Salmigondis: Contes de toutes les couleurs*.

December

16 (Sun)   MWS has received an £80 bill for Percy's first quarter at Harrow – about twice as much as she was led to expect. She asks Gregson to put her case to Sir Timothy, but he (through Gregson, in a letter of 3 January), refuses to assist her. She is anxious that Percy should not have to leave the school – he is happy there and to leave now would be a slur on his reputation – and so decides, to save on fees, that she should move to Harrow and Percy become a 'home boarder'.

1833

Carey, Lea and Blanchard of Philadelphia publish their unauthorized two-volume edition of *The Last Man*.

MWS's 'The Smuggler and his Family' is included in *Original Compositions in Prose and Verse*. The name 'Mrs Shelley' is printed in the list of contents instead of the usual 'Author of *Frankenstein*' or anonymity.

January

1 (Tues)   MWS, Godwin, and Leicester Stanhope are among guests at the Woods'.

16   *Lodore* is nearly finished. MWS sends Ollier the first volume on 31.

16   Trelawny sails for America.

February

She reads and finds 'beautiful' Godwin's *Deloraine* (Journals, p. 186).

March

Julia and Rosa Robinson stay with MWS. On 12 (Tues) they are joined for dinner by Joshua Robinson, Godwin, and Major Aubrey Beauclerk.

Probably this month, with Sir Timothy still proving obdurate, John Gregson personally loans MWS £50, to be repaid by deductions from her next two quarterly advances.

April

MWS and Percy have influenza and on 15 (Mon) Lady Paul dies of it. She and Sir John Paul have been furnishing for MWS the house in Harrow to which she is about to move.

22	The Godwins visit; on 24 MWS and Percy visit them.
c. 26	She moves to Harrow, which she soon comes to find, especially without Lady Paul's anticipated companionship, dull and inhospitable (Letters, ii. 208).

She anticipates a change (Journals, p. 529), probably because she is in love with Aubrey Beauclerk and hopes that they will marry. (For discussion of the evidence about this relationship see Letters, ii.184, Sunstein, pp. 316, 321–2, and Seymour, pp. 425–6.) *Clairmont Correspondence* ii.357, n.6, points out that in the 1870s CC claims, in conversation with the Shelley enthusiast Edward Silsbee, that Beauclerk proposed marriage to MWS and was accepted, but she withdrew when his family expressed doubts about her financial position.

May

4 (Sat)	Following Godwin's appointment as Yeoman Usher of the Receipt of the Exchequer, he and Mary Jane Godwin move into their free accommodation at 13 New Palace Yard. MWS feels that she no longer needs to worry about their finances. Partly because of this and perhaps more so because of her hopes of Beauclerk, this is 'the only genial spring I ever knew' (Journals, p. 529).
10	She visits the Godwins in their new home.

June

9 (Sun)	Her influenza returns. She does not fully recover until August.

July
Julia Robinson comes to stay.

29 (Mon)   MWS sends the manuscript of 'The Mortal Immortal' to *The Keepsake* (see November).

August
MWS and Percy stay with the Robinsons at 2 Melbury Terrace, Dorset Square, Putney, for much of this month and several weeks of September. In Journal entries for these months she talks of dark night, calamity, and misfortune, almost certainly because she has learned that Beauclerk intends to marry Ida Goring. She is soothed (Journals, p. 530) by the friendship of Gee Paul, Beauclerk's sister.

September
This month MWS possibly attends a debate at the House of Commons. (See 'Newly Uncovered Letters and Poems', p. 65.)

2 (Mon)   Further Harrow expenses force MWS to ask Gregson to let her defer until Christmas repayment of the £25 she still owes him.

10   She dates her poem 'Fair Italy! Still shines thy sun as bright …' ('Newly Uncovered Letters and Poems', pp. 73–4).

c. 26   She returns to Harrow.

27   MWS goes to a party at the Manners-Suttons' and visits the Godwins. Godwin goes back to Harrow with her on 28 and stays overnight. Jane Williams Hogg also visits.

October
10 (Thurs) She dines at Greenhill, near Harrow, with Sir John Paul and his children John Paul and Mary-Horatia Bankhead.

14   Julia Robinson comes to stay (until 23 November), joined at some point by her sister Ellen.

24   MWS, Godwin, and Gabriele Rossetti are at the Stanhopes'.

November
Between now and April 1834 she sends *Lodore* to the press in short sections.

'The Mortal Immortal: a Tale', by 'the Author of *Frankenstein*', is in *The Keepsake for MDCCCXXXIV*.

14 (Fri)   She feels she ought to be content but is beset by memories and vague fears (Journals, pp. 531–2).

Soon after 21, at her request, Ollier sends her books which have recently been published by Bentley: Horace Walpole's letters and Lady Charlotte Maria Bury's *Trevelyan*.

23   MWS is copying PBS's letters, presumably with an eventual edition in mind. She is also about to begin work on lives of Italian writers for Rev. Dionysius Lardner's *Lives of the Most Eminent Literary and Scientific Men of Italy, Spain and Portugal*. She may have been recommended to Lardner by Moore.

December
2 (Mon)   She goes to London, staying probably with the Robinsons at Putney. She visits the Stanhopes on 3 and her father on 4. On 5 she dines with Cecilia Gore, daughter of the novelist Catherine Gore, on 6 sees Jane Williams Hogg and, with Julia Robinson, dines with Trelawny's daughter Julia, now Mrs Burley. MWS hopes that all this company will help 'soften the pangs of Memory' (Journals, p. 535).
7   She returns to Harrow.

At about mid-month she is in London again, staying with Julia Burley. MWS sees her elderly aunt, Everina Wollstonecraft, who has moved to Pentonville and needs financial assistance. MWS finds her assuming and disagreeable.

1834

Carey, Lea and Blanchard of Philadelphia publish their unauthorized two-volume edition of *Perkin Warbeck*. Probably this year, MWS corrects a copy of the first edition of the novel with a second edition in mind. (In 1857 Routledge issues a reprint of the first edition.)

This year MWS perhaps meets Benjamin Disraeli, whom she certainly knows by late 1837 (see Letters, ii.290, n.1).

'The Swiss Peasant', by 'Mrs Shelley', is reprinted in *The Tale Book*, First Series, in Baudry's European Library, Paris.

January
8 (Wed)   MWS goes to London with her aunt.
c. 20   Edward Moxon approaches MWS about the possibility of publishing an edition of PBS's work. She explains that

'family reasons' (see August 1824) make this impossible
at present, but expresses interest for the future.

February

13 (Thurs)   Marriage of Aubrey Beauclerk and Ida Goring. MWS
writes 'Farewell' in her Journal, where on 16 she notes
that calm has succeeded the first sorrow. She remains,
however, evidently depressed.

March

6 (Thurs)   She is in London and sees her father.

15   She has been reading Catherine Gore's *The Hamiltons*
and Bulwer's *Godolphin*.

April

Early this month thirty-six pages of the *Lodore* manuscript, of which
there is no other copy, are lost in the post. At some point after 30
(Wed) she rewrites them. Work on the Italian lives also continues.

May

She visits London, returning to Harrow on 24 (Sat) with Mary-
Horatia Bankhead.

June

At about the beginning of this month she is in London again,
attempting unsuccessfully to arrange a new financial settlement
with her father-in-law through Gregson.

7 (Sat)   She sends off the rewritten section of *Lodore*.

23   Having received a copy of the title-page, MWS
expresses doubts about the subtitle of *Lodore – A Tale of
the Present Time* and suggests to Ollier that Godwin
should be consulted. Perhaps on his advice, the title
becomes simply *Lodore*.

July

8 (Tues)   The twelfth anniversary of PBS's death; since then
MWS's life has been 'one tissue of adversity'. Her son
Percy is 'the only flower that adorns the gloomy
expanse'. She has received only 'one little note' from
Beauclerk. Work on the Italian literary lives, however,
helps to calm her (Journals, p. 539 and n.1).

17	She has finished her lives of Petrarch and Boccaccio and is now working on Machiavelli.
17	She tells Maria Gisborne about fourteen-year-old Percy, clearly no intellectual compared with his parents, but very loving towards her (Letters, ii. 209). She discusses him further in letters to Gisborne on 19 August and 30 October.
24	Death of Coleridge.
29	MWS and Percy come to London, staying at 7 Upper Eaton Street. They visit Godwin frequently.

August
11 (Mon)	MWS is at the House of Lords to hear debates on the Irish tithe question and the new Poor Law.
13	She goes to Douglas Jerrold's *Beau Nash* at the Haymarket.
19	*Lodore* has been printed but publication is delayed.
30	She dines with the Manners-Suttons.

September
2 (Tues)	Cecilia Gore visits MWS.
c. 15	MWS and Percy return to Harrow at the end of his school holidays.

November
17 (Mon)	She is reading a translation of Anselm von Feurbach's *Kaspar Hauser*.

MWS publishes her 'The Elder Son' in *Heath's Book of Beauty for 1835* (by 'Mrs Shelley') and 'The Trial of Love' in *The Keepsake for MDCC-CXXXV* (as 'the Author of *Frankenstein*'). 'The False Rhyme' is reprinted in *The American Keepsake: a Christmas and New-Year's Offering, 1835.*

December
2 (Tues)	In a long Journal entry she reflects on topics including her solitude, unluckiness in friendship, love for Percy, and imagination. Her 'querulous' Journals, she says, give an imperfect picture of her because they record not her imagination but her feelings. The Italian lives, she says,

have saved her life and reason. She writes in the mornings and reads novels and memoirs in the evenings.

15   MWS writes 'To the Dead', later published as 'Stanzas' ('O come to me in dreams, my love!') – see 1838.

27   Charles Lamb dies.

30   She writes to Ollier to ask what has happened to 'lost Lodore'.

1835

'Transformation', by 'Mrs Shelley', is reprinted in *The Tale Book*, Second Series, in Baudry's European Library, Paris.

January
Now or in February the publisher Edward Moxon offers MWS £600 for an edition and life of PBS.

29 (Thurs) Death of Mrs Mason. MWS hears the news about a month later.

February
At the beginning of this month the first volume of Lardner's *Lives of the Most Eminent Literary and Scientific Men of Italy, Spain and Portugal* is published by Longman, Orme, Brown. MWS is the author of the sections on Petrarch, Boccaccio, Machiavelli, Lorenzo de' Medici, Ficino, Pico della Mirandola, Politian, Cieco da Ferrara, Burchiello, Boiardo, Berni, and Bernardo, Luca and Luigi Pulci. (She states in letters to Hunt and Gisborne – Letters, ii. 219, 222 – that all but the lives of Dante and Ariosto are hers.) Hard work on the lives this winter has contributed to another period of depression (Journals, p. 546).

2 (Mon)   Jane Williams Hogg and her mother, Mary Cleveland, visit MWS.

9   She is reading Giambattista Marino's *L'Adone*.

20   Murray has sent her a copy of *Finden's Illustrations of the Life and Works of Lord Byron* and probably, as requested on 10, the 'prospectus' of the new Murray edition of Boswell's *Life of Johnson*. She has read the Life many times, finds it the 'most amusing' of books, and loves Johnson 'the kind hearted wise & Gentle Bear' (Letters, ii.223).

Following the failure of Sir Charles Manners-Sutton to be re-elected as Speaker of the House of Commons on 19, MWS feels cooler towards the Whigs than formerly, although she 'supposes' she is one (Letters, ii.223). She feels correspondingly sympathetic to the Tories, not least because the Duke of Wellington and Sir Robert Peel intervened to prevent the abolition of Godwin's post as Yeoman Usher.

March

2 (Mon) – *c.* 7 MWS is in London, as again between about 11 and 24. As on subsequent visits over the next few months she sees her father often. On 2 she is with him at the Stanhopes'. She also briefly sees Moore.

17   Probable date of MWS's first meeting with Sydney, Lady Morgan.

25   She tells Ollier that she wishes copies of *Lodore* to be sent to Peacock, Godwin, Viscountess Canterbury (Ellen Manners-Sutton), Mrs Stanhope, and Gee Paul. She is reading Lady Stepney's *The Heir Presumptive*.

April

3 (Fri)   She writes to Gabriele Rossetti to inquire about sources for her lives of Alfieri and Monti. She writes again on 20 to ask Rossetti if he could arrange for her to meet his father-in-law, Gaetano Polidori, who was Alfieri's secretary. (John William Polidori was the son of Gaetano.) It is unknown when or whether she meets him.

7   MWS's *Lodore*, 'By the Author of *Frankenstein*' is published, in three volumes, by Richard Bentley. This year three unauthorized editions of the novel are also published, by Wallis and Newell (New York), Galignani (Paris), and Wahlen (Brussels). Reviews are generally favourable. On 16 the *Courier*, for instance, praises this 'more natural' successor to her earlier 'wild fictions' and on 19 the *Sunday Times* describes it as 'an affecting tale of domestic affections and every-day life'. CC, however, objects, when she writes to MWS on 15 March 1836, to Lodore's evidently Byronic characteristics; 'that vile spirit' – as Castruccio, Raymond, Lodore – haunts the pages of all her novels except *Frankenstein* (Clairmont Correspondence, ii.341).

15   She is in London, as again on *c*. 25–28 (staying at 7 Upper Eaton Street).

May
c. 12 (Tues) – 17 She comes to London again. She feels ill and returns to Harrow.
c. 23   She has been reading Caroline Norton's *'The Wife' and 'Woman's Reward'*.
26   MWS meets William Charles Macready at Dr Lardner's. Others present include Caroline Norton, the Stanhopes, and the journalist Albany Fonblanque (Macready's *Diaries*, i.229–30).

June
11 (Sun)   She has been reading John Gisborne's 'Evelina'. Its length and her lack of suitable contacts mean that she will not be able to find a publisher for it. MWS can only write poetry, if at all, she tells Maria Gisborne in the same letter, under the influence of strong feeling; she could once, but no longer, have written a good tragedy. But she has always been a 'dependant thing', in need of support, and feels that women are, in the end, better but weaker and less intellectual than men (Letters, ii.245–6).

Some time this month or the next MWS, ill, depressed, or both, sends urgently for Jane Williams Hogg, who looks after her for some time (Letters, ii.249, n.1).

July
Trelawny arrives back from America.
23 (Thurs) The Godwins visit Harrow. Julia Robinson, who has recently returned after a long period in Brussels, is there too.
29   MWS is in London and visits the Godwins.

August
c. 1 (Sat) MWS and Percy go to Dover, where they stay at 3 Alfred Place. By 6 she feels that she is regaining her strength (see June); she relapses for a time, however, in the autumn. They probably remain in Dover, where they are

in company with Trelawny's mother Maria Brereton, and daughter Julia Burley, until the first week of September.

September
6 (Sun) – 22 MWS is in London. She sees much of her father.

At about the end of the month she is away from Harrow for a few days visiting the Stanhopes, the Robinsons at Putney, and Maria Brereton at Brompton.
This month and next she is involved in negotiations on Trelawny's behalf following the unexpected announcement of a reissue of *Adventures of a Younger Son* in Bentley's Standard Novels. A settlement is finally achieved in May 1836.

October
Probably this month the second volume of the Italian, Spanish, and Portuguese *Lives* is published. MWS is the author of the sections on Guicciardini, Vittoria Colonna, Guarini, Chiabrera, Tassoni, Marino, Filicaia, Metastasio, Goldoni, Alfieri, Monti, and Foscolo.
3 (Sat)   She is having difficulty obtaining material for the Spanish and Portuguese lives she is now researching. She is stimulated, however, by this treading in unknown paths, and wishes she could go to Spain (Letters, ii.255).

Following the success of *Lodore* Ollier wants her to write another novel for Bentley.

November
6 (Fri)   The Godwins move to the Exchequer Building, Whitehall Yard.
8   MWS tells Maria Gisborne that she increasingly feels fidelity to be the most important of human virtues and that she is going to write a novel on this theme (*Falkner*).

December
3 (Thurs) Thomas Moore writes, on MWS's behalf, to ask Lady Holland about possible access to her husband's Spanish library. Frustratingly, but as expected, the request is politely refused.

1836

January
Death of John Gisborne.

18 (Mon) – 23 MWS is in London.

25   She has finished writing the first volume of *Falkner*. It is
          in the same style as *Lodore* but the story is more interest-
          ing and, she thinks, more popular; she expects to be paid
          more this time, she tells Ollier (Letters, ii.263).
          Eventually she will publish the novel not with Bentley
          but with Saunders and Otley, who are willing to pay her
          an advance (Letters, ii.280).

February
4 (Thurs) Birth of MWS's goddaughter, Prudentia Sarah Hogg.

March
c. 23 (Wed) MWS and Percy leave Harrow and move to 14 North
          Bank, Regent's Park, London. They dine with Godwin.
          Percy is to study, with five other young men, with a
          tutor, Rev. Archibald Morrison, Vicar of Stoneleigh in
          Warwickshire.

April
7 (Thurs) Death of William Godwin. MWS has been with him for
          much of the last few days, and is ill for a time afterwards.

Maria Gisborne dies a few days after Godwin.

14   Godwin's funeral. He is buried near his first wife in St
          Pancras churchyard. The mourners include MWS, Percy,
          Thomas Campbell, James Kenney, and Trelawny, who
          has helped to arrange the interment. Godwin's will asks
          his daughter to sort through his manuscripts.

Soon after the funeral Percy goes to live with Morrison at Stoneleigh
for a term (ending on 2 July).

May
21 (Sat)   MWS sees Moore.

June

She is still writing *Falkner* and believes it will be her best novel (Journals, p. 548). But she contrasts her real misery with the tranquillity with which others, including Godwin, have conjured up 'fictitious woes'. She feels that her health is 'irremediably shattered'. Some time between 8 (Wed) June and 24 August she moves to 4 Lower Belgrave Street, London.

11   What purports to be a conversation with MWS is published in 'Lord Byron and his Contemporaries, &c., by an Intimate Friend of his Lordship. – No. III', *Metropolitan Literary Journal of Literature, Science, the Fine Arts, &c.*, no. 10, pp. 151–4.

July

19 (Tues) Colburn agrees to pay 350 guineas to Mary Jane Godwin, now in need of support once more, for an edition by MWS of Godwin's unfinished memoirs and his correspondence. (MWS and Caroline Norton also work to persuade the prime minister, Lord Melbourne, to grant the widow £300.) This summer she writes to Josiah Wedgwood and William Hazlitt, Jr, amongst others, to ask for any publishable Godwin letters in their possession. She still appears to be working on the project in May 1840 (Seymour, 455) but does not bring it to completion, partly because of illness and work on her PBS editions.

October

c. 10 (Mon) MWS goes to Brighton in the hope of recovering from the illness and low spirits which have dogged her for the last eighteen months or so (Journals, pp. 549–50).

November

CC comes to London but moves to Windsor with her current employers, the Bennets, soon afterwards.

MWS, as 'Mrs Shelley', publishes her story 'The Parvenue' in *The Keepsake for MDCCCXXXVII*.

December

Probably this month Caroline Norton sends MWS the draft of her *Observations on the Natural Claim of a Mother to the Custody of Her*

Young Children (1837). (Norton has separated from her husband, who has retained custody of their three children.) MWS replies, by 5 January, with comments drawn on or incorporated in the final version of the text.

Falkner is finished by the end of the year. Its completion has been delayed by MWS's persistent ill-health (Letters, ii. 280).

1837

January

26 (Thurs) She tells Trelawny that she will write her father's life but must delay it for the sake of Percy's prospects and reputation, which would be adversely affected if attention were drawn to Godwin's views on religion. No doubt for the same reason she fails to publish his last work *The Genius of Christianity Unveiled* (Seymour, pp. 452–4).

February

Saunders and Otley publish MWS's *Falkner. A Novel*, 'By the Author of *Frankenstein, The Last Man*, etc', in three volumes. The same publishers reprint the work in New York. *Falkner* is on the whole well received. According to the *Monthly Review* for March MWS 'seems ... to have imbibed much of her husband's poetic temperament, its singular loveliness and delicacy, but to have shorn it of those extravagant visions and emotions which led him beyond the province of truth'. MWS herself tells Hunt, on 26 April, that *Falkner* is a favourite of hers, although she feels that it has suffered from being written too fast and concentrated too much on one topic (Letters, ii.285–6).

2 (Thurs)   She returns to London from Brighton.

March

She moves to 24 South Audley Street, London.

At Easter (Easter Day is 26) she stays with Gee Paul in Sussex.

June

This summer MWS possibly meets Frances Kemble Butler (Fanny Kemble).

1 (Thurs)   She is working on the life of Cervantes.

Some time after 1 she visits Brighton. She is there on 20 and returns to London by 30.

20   King William IV dies and is succeeded by Queen Victoria.

July
3 (Mon) and 13 MWS asks John Bowring for material on several of the Spanish authors and works to be considered in the *Lives*.
7   Percy Florence Shelley is admitted at Trinity College, Cambridge.

August
7 (Mon)   MWS and Moore are at Caroline Norton's.
30   MWS's fortieth birthday.

October
About now the third volume of Lardner's Italian, Spanish and Portuguese *Lives* is published. MWS provides introductory material and lives of Boscán, Garcilaso de la Vega, Diego Hurtado de Mendoza, Luis de León, Herrera, Montemayor, Castillejo, Ercilla, Cervantes, Lope de Vega, Espinel, Villegas, Góngora, Quevedo, Calderón, Ribeyra, Sá de Miranda, Gil Vicente, Ferreira, and Camoëns. MWS is now working on French lives, which she finds less interesting than the Spanish and Portuguese but which are pleasant and easy enough to write and supply some small amount of 'the *needful*' (Letters, ii. 293).
c. 10 (Tues) Percy begins his first term at Trinity College, Cambridge.

November
MWS may be the author of a story, 'The Pilgrims', in *The Keepsake for MDCCCXXXVIII*.
She moves to 41d Park Street, Grosvenor Square, London.
By this autumn Augusta Goring often sees MWS. They were introduced by Trelawny in 1836.
Some time between this month and March 1839 she sends Lady Morgan a lock of Byron's hair: see Letters, ii.294 and n.1.

December
4 (Mon)   Peacock's daughter Mary Ellen visits MWS.
31   This year she has been happier than usual; correspondence with the loyal Julia Robinson, now in Ireland, has helped to support her (Journals, p. 551).

1838

MWS knows Richard Monckton Milnes by December this year (see Letters, ii.303, n.4).

February

A version of MWS may figure briefly as 'Mrs Godwin Percy' in John H. Hunt's 'Luigi Rivarola: a Tale of Modern Italy', in the *Young Lady's Magazine*, vol. 10, pp. 71–2 (W. H. Lyles, *Mary Shelley: an Annotated Bibliography*, 1975, p. 205).

15 (Wed)   Today or soon afterwards MWS sees Bulwer's *The Lady of Lyons* at Covent Garden. She writes enthusiastically to him about the naturalness of the dialogue and action; he shows promise of becoming a great dramatic writer (Letters, ii.295). They have talked recently.

March

3 (Sat)   MWS's life of Voltaire has been printed and her life of Rousseau is at the press.

12   She dates her song 'O listen while I sing to thee'.

April

Percy has fallen in love, probably with the otherwise uncertainly identified Gertrude to whom he has 'engaged himself' by February 1839 (Journals, p. 562). MWS regards her as unsuitable in some way. (See Clairmont Correspondence, pp. 350, 353).

23 (Mon)   Death of Ida Goring Beauclerk, Aubrey Beauclerk's wife.

May

14 (Mon)   MWS's life of La Fontaine is at the press and she has finished work on Pascal ('Newly Uncovered Letters and Poems', p. 67).

June

3 (Sun)   Moore calls.

30   MWS and Rosa Robinson are at one of Samuel Rogers's famous breakfast gatherings. She has had too little of such 'intellectual fascinating society' (Journals, p. 553).

This summer Augusta Goring goes to live near Trelawny in Putney (they will later marry), effectively ending her friendship with MWS.

July
Probably this month the first volume of Lardner's *Lives of the Most Eminent Literary and Scientific Men of France* is published by Longman, Orme, Brown. MWS writes on Montaigne, Rabelais, Corneille, Rochefoucauld, Molière, La Fontaine, Pascal, Mme de Sévigné, Boileau, Racine, and Fénelon.

August
c. 3 (Fri) or 4 MWS writes to Sir Timothy Shelley to ask if, since there have been several pirate editions, she can now bring out an edition of PBS's works. He agrees, with the provision that no life of the poet will be included; she does, however, write notes on the history of the poems which enable her to provide biographical information.

9   MWS, Henry Crabb Robinson, and Joseph Severn are among Rogers's breakfast guests.

October
6 (Sat)   She is at Drury Lane with Eliza Robinson and, probably, Richard Rothwell.

21   She writes an unusually long entry (Journals, pp. 553–9) analysing the reasons why she cannot speak out publicly on behalf of women's rights and other reformist causes. She respects people who, like her parents and PBS, try to reform the world but with real disinterest, tolerance, and understanding; she, however, is 'not a person of Opinions'. She feels she lacks ability in argument, is unsure of her views on the position of women, and can often see both sides of an issue. She dislikes the violence of the Radicals. She likes society; 'living intercourse' does more than books. If she has not written on the rights of women, she has always befriended and helped oppressed women, victims of the social system. Journals, p. 558, n.1, suggests that these comments are a response to criticism by Trelawny for not, with him, supporting the Philosophical Radicals.

November
2 (Wed)   'A Tale of the Passions' (see 6 November 1822 and 1 January 1823) is reprinted, as the work of 'Mrs Shelley',

in the first volume of *The Romancist, and Novelist's Library: The Best Works of the Best Authors*, edited by William Hazlitt, Jr, who asks, some time between 2 and 5, whether *Frankenstein* would also be available. (See 30 June 1831.) She orders her weekly copy of *The Romancist*, which costs only twopence.

'Euphrasia: a Tale of Greece', by 'Mrs Shelley', 'Stanzas' beginning 'How like a star you rose upon my life' and 'Stanzas' beginning 'O come to me in dreams, my love!' (see 15 December 1834) are published in *The Keepsake for MDCCCXXXIX*.

December

3 (Mon)   She is at Lady Morgan's party with Rogers and the American politician Charles Sumner. She tells Sumner that 'the greatest happiness for any woman [is] to be the wife or mother of a distinguished man' (see Letters, ii.305–6, n.2).

7   MWS has agreed with Moxon for the publication of *The Poetical Works of Percy Bysshe Shelley*. By January 1839 he has also agreed to pay her £500 for the copyright.

11   Moxon has suggested omitting 'atheistical' matter from *Queen Mab*. In public MWS is inclined to agree that anything 'irreligious' should be avoided, but in February 1839 says that she '*much* disliked the leaving out of any of Queen Mab' (Journals, p. 560). Before deciding to go ahead with the expurgation, she has to work hard to find a copy of the poem as originally printed (Letters, ii.301–4).

12   She asks Moxon for Wordsworth, Southey and Coleridge editions. (When she receives them in May 1839, however, she finds the Southey too expensive and sends it back.)

14   She politely but firmly refuses Hunt's offer to help with the notes for the PBS edition.

1839

Late in 1838 or early in 1839 MWS is at Woodley in Berkshire for a holiday.

January

17 (Thurs) Possible date when Sumner sees MWS again. He admires the graceful way she addresses French and Italian guests in their respective languages (Letters ii.308, n.1).

c. 18 She reassures Moore that PBS appreciated his poetry, especially his songs and short poems.

25 She probably (Letters, ii.309) entertains guests including Jane Williams Hogg and Mary Ellen Peacock.

By 26 the first volume of *The Poetical Works of Percy Bysshe Shelley*, 'edited by Mrs Shelley', is published by Moxon. The remaining three volumes are published in early March, April, and the beginning of May. MWS's omissions from *Queen Mab* are much criticised. Hogg's complaint about her leaving out the dedication to Harriet particularly angers her; as she tells him on 11 February she omitted it in deference to PBS' stated views. Trelawny sends his copy of volume 1 back to Moxon; no doubt he enjoys the opportunity 'to do a rude & insolent act' (Journals, p. 560).

February

Some time after this month Percy's involvement with Gertrude (see April 1838) ends.

March

4 (Mon) Henry Crabb Robinson sees MWS and Percy and finds him 'a loutish-looking boy, quite unworthy of his intellectual ancestors in appearance' (*On Books and their Writers*, p. 569).

Some time after 18 she borrows a copy of *The Winter's Wreath* (1824) in order to consult her *Proserpine*.

c. 25 MWS leaves Park Street and moves to Layton House, Upper Richmond Road, Putney. Here she sees the Stanhopes and, now living along the river at Kew, the Robinsons. She does not, however, see Trelawny or Augusta Goring in Putney (see Letters, ii.319). The main aim of the move is to recuperate, in country surroundings, from the nervous exhaustion which MWS suffers under the strain of working on the PBS edition. For a time she feels on the verge of insanity (Journals, p. 563).

'Recurrence to the past, full of its own deep and unfor-gotten joys and sorrows, contrasted with succeeding years of painful and solitary struggle, has shaken my health' and, she believes, influenced her notes for the worse ('Note on Shelley's Poems of 1822' in *Poetical Works*.) She may, however, be suffering the first symp-toms of the slow brain tumour which will eventually kill her. Julia Robinson helps her through her illness.

April

4 (Thurs) Moxon sends MWS Harriet Martineau's recently pub-lished *Deerbrook*. It lacks Jane Austen's humour, but equals her in vividness and is more philosophical. MWS also orders Henry Taylor's *Philip van Artevelde* and the new edition of Thomas Campbell's *Poetical Works* from Moxon.

May

2 (Thurs) MWS writes to Edward Moxon to propose an edition of PBS's prose. She begins to work on this probably in June (Letters, ii.316). The work, she tells Hunt, is not as painful to her as was that on the poems (Letters, ii.319).

June

19 (Wed) She breakfasts at Samuel Rogers' with Moore, Julia or Rosa Robinson, and the Stanhopes. The conversation, according to Moore, is mainly about the Bulwers' quar-rels. Literary people are the worst society, he concludes, but MWS is an exception 'for she is at least feminine'.

July

Late this month she works on revises for the second volume of French *Lives*.

20 (Sat) She asks Peacock, through his daughter, to send his manuscripts of PBS's *Defence of Poetry* and *Symposium* for the prose edition (Letters, ii.317); she asks again on 29 August. This summer she also gathers PBS letters from various correspondents.

c. 22–25 She probably sees Jane Williams Hogg (Letters, ii.318).

31 Possible date of a visit from Hunt (Letters, ii.319–20). Some of the Robinsons are also expected.

August

1 (Thurs) Publication of the second volume of French *Lives*. MWS
writes on Voltaire, Rousseau, Condorcet, Mirabeau, Mme
Roland, and Mme de Staël.

September

Early this month the physician and geologist Gideon Mantell sends
her one of his books, perhaps *Wonders of Geology* (1838) (Letters,
ii.324, n.1).

c.5 (Thurs)-18 She is in Sussex.

October

2 (Wed) Hunt, Campbell, and Moxon are invited to dine today.

8 After consultation with Hunt MWS decides to withdraw
PBS's 'On the Devil and Devils' from the prose edition.

11 She is correcting the proofs of PBS's translation of
Plato's *Ion*.

By 23 she knows Thomas and Jane Welsh Carlyle. She is perhaps
introduced to them by Hunt (Journals, p. 329, n.4) or meets Thomas
Carlyle at one of Rogers's breakfasts (Seymour, p. 459).

November

11 (Mon) The second edition of PBS's *Poetical Works* is published,
dated 1840. Alterations include the restoration of material cut from *Queen Mab*.

27 MWS expresses qualified hope of at least being a comfort
to the widowed Aubrey Beauclerk; 'but will not events
place us asunder[?]' (Journals, p. 564).

December

3 (Tues) Thomas Carlyle sends MWS, who is looking for an epi-
graph for the PBS prose edition, a copy of his translation
from Goethe, *Wilhelm Meister's Apprenticeship and Travels*.
Soon afterwards *Essays, Letters from Abroad, Translations
and Fragments, by Percy Bysshe Shelley* (Moxon, '1840'),
'edited by Mrs Shelley', is published in two volumes. It
includes a revision of *Six Weeks' Tour* as 'Journal of a Six
Weeks' Tour' and 'Letters from Geneva'.

19 She is angered by a review of *Essays, Letters* in the
Spectator of 14 which attacks the choice and quality of

	the works; her taste harmonizes 'with the weakest and most defective parts of [PBS's] mind'.
21	Abraham Hayward, lawyer, author and gastronome, visits MWS.
c. 23	She refuses, through Hunt, to help or approve George Henry Lewes in his proposed biography of PBS. She herself cannot write his life and cannot talk even to close friends about the 'tragical' reasons for this; all the less, therefore, can she discuss such matters with a stranger. She cannot yet remove the seal from the fountain (Letters, ii.334–5).

About now she asks Ollier whether Bentley would consider publishing *Valperga* in his Standard Novels series.

Probably late this year (Seymour, pp. 457, 569) she sits for a portrait by Richard Rothwell, now in the National Portrait Gallery.

1840

January
6 (Mon)	She praises the simplicity and melodiousness of poems by Campbell, whose works she has just received from Moxon.
15	Probable date of a gathering at MWS's where the guests include Hunt and several of Percy's friends, among them his Trinity friend Alexander Knox.

February
3 (Mon)	By this date CC is living in London. (She moves to Paris in 1841.)
7	MWS, Percy, and Richard Rothwell are at the first night of Hunt's *A Legend of Florence* at Covent Garden. She possibly also meets George Henry Lewes on this occasion (see Letters, iii.14, n.1).
20 or 21	Moore, MWS, Julia and Rosa Robinson, and Colonel Jeremiah Ratcliffe (whom MWS has known since the autumn of 1837 or earlier) dine at Rogers's.

March
3 (Fri)	Police officers prevent a duel between Louis Napoleon Bonaparte and Count Léon. The scandal which results

for Colonel Ratcliffe, Léon's second, is one factor in the disturbance which leads to his being placed in a mental asylum. MWS several times expresses grief and agitation at the fate of her friend.

4   MWS and friends, probably including Elizabeth Stanhope and Abraham Hayward, go to Hunt's *A Legend* again.

25   She moves to 3 The Rise, Richmond, near the river for Percy's boating. The Robinsons are nearby at Kew.

April

Rothwell's portrait of MWS goes on show at the Royal Academy exhibition. Probably he later gives or sells it to her.

June

c. 1 (Fri)   MWS moves to 20 Rock Gardens, Brighton. She is joined by Percy after the end of his Cambridge term on 6, in preparation for their trip to the Continent.

1   Soothed by a balmy, moonlit evening, she heads a Journal entry 'amore redivivus'. She has been burdened by ill-health and depression and believes (as she says several times in letters also) that she somehow brings misfortune to her friends, but on a night like this she feels the presence of loving spirits, perhaps including the 'beloved dead' (Journals, pp. 564–5).

13   MWS, her maid Marianne, and Percy sail from Dover to Calais. On arrival in Paris on 15 they stay at Hôtel Chatham. They probably see Lady Canterbury and Aubrey Beauclerk's brother Charles (*Novels and Selected Works*, 8.80, n.a). The party is joined by Percy's friends George Hibbert Deffell and Julian Robinson, brother of Julia, Rosa, Eliza and Isabel. Later (possibly on 28 July – see *Novels and Selected Works*, 8.113, n.a) Robert Leslie Ellis joins the party.

25   They travel from Paris to Metz (27) via Châlons-sur-Marne, Clermont, and Verdun – 'by far the most agreeable part of France I had ever traversed' (*Novels and Selected Works*, 8.82). They go on to Trier (28) and by boat down the Moselle to Piesport (29), Bernkastel, and Cochem (30).

July

1 (Wed)   They reach Koblenz (Hôtel Belle Vue), from which they go by Rhine steamer to Mainz (2) and by rail to Frankfurt-am-Main (3). By carriage they reach Darmstadt, Heidelberg (4), which has 'an ancient, picturesque, inartificial look, more consonant with our ideas of German romance' than towns they have passed through recently, Karlsruhe (5), Baden-Baden (6), Offenburg, Ettenheim (8), Stein (9 – *Novels and Selected Works*, 8.99, n.6), the Black Forest, Freiburg, Schaffhausen and its falls (10), Zürich, where they stay at the Hôtel du Lac (11), Chur (12), the Via Mala gorge, Splügen, Chiavenna (13), Colico, and by steamer across Lake Como to Cadenabbia (14), where they stay at the Albergo Grande.

19   A sailing-boat ordered locally by Percy arrives and expeditions on Lake Como commence. At first this makes MWS highly nervous but she learns at least not to show her fear.

August

10 (Mon)   The group spends an evening on the lake. They enjoy performances of poetry – Manzoni's Ode on Napoleon is recited – and music. As well as boating MWS visits Bellagio a number of times, Villa Serbelloni, Villa Melzi, Como for a production of Donizetti's *Lucia di Lammermoor* (before 15), and Villa Sommariva, where she finds Canova's *Cupid and Psyche* awkward in comparison with Greek sculpture. In Cadenabbia she reads Italian works, especially Dante and Tasso.

18   She records her joy at life on Lake Como and the shadow cast by her dread of returning to rain, isolation and poverty in England (Journals, pp. 565–8). She is also very probably hoping for a letter from Aubrey Beauclerk.

30   She feels happy and in good spirits today, her birthday (Journals, p. 569).

September

9 (Wed)   They go to Lecco and then to Bergamo, where they stay at an unpleasant inn and hear Rossini's *Mosè in Egitto*.

MWS appreciates Rossini 'having been of late confined to Donizetti'; *Mosè* is 'rich in impressive and even sublime vocal effects' (*Novels and Selected Works*, 8.130–1).

11   They travel to Hôtel de la Ville, Milan. She sees and is impressed by Leonardo's *Last Supper*, and sees the Brera, the Biblioteca Ambrosiana, and a silk factory. She goes to Otto Nicolai's *Il Templario* at La Scala. On 13 she is at mass in the cathedral.

18   Percy and his friends set off for England. MWS stays on because money she expected has apparently failed to arrive. In the mornings she visits the cathedral. The money eventually appears on 27.

29   MWS and Marianne leave Milan. On 29 they reach Arona; MWS admires the colossal statue of San Carlo Borromeo. On 30 she visits the islands of Lake Maggiore and Baveno and reaches Domodossola.

October

1 (Thurs)   She crosses the Simplon pass and goes on to Sion (2), Vevey (3) and, by steamer, Geneva (4), staying at Hôtel de Bergues. As she passes along the lake she sees Villa Diodati and Maison Chappuis; 'Was I the same person who had lived there, the companion of the dead?' (*Novels and Selected Works*, 8.148).

She reaches Lyon on 6. In Paris, from 10, she stays briefly at Hôtel Chatham. Charles Beauclerk then lends her his third-floor rooms at rue de la Paix 15 while he returns to England. On 26 she tells Hayward that she likes travelling more than anything else.

In Paris she sees Lord and Lady Canterbury (the Manners-Suttons), the Boinville-Turner family, and Byron's friend Scrope Davies. She meets Charles Augustin Sainte-Beuve. She may also meet Alphonse de Lamartine (Letters, iii.333, n.2) and, in November or later, the journalist Jean-Alexandre Buchon. General Guglielmo Pepè asks her to try to have his work on modern Italy published in England (see 'Newly Uncovered Letters and Poems', pp. 68–9 and Letters, iii.14 and n.3). Paris is no substitute for 'Italy and sunshine' (Letters, iii.11) but is evidently preferable to London.

November

MWS receives, in a letter from CC, the no doubt disappointing news that Aubrey Beauclerk is to marry Rosa Robinson.

5 (Thurs)   She watches King Louis-Philippe addressing the Chamber of Deputies and is moved by his tears when describing an attempt on his life.

8   Some time after this date (Letters, iii.7) MWS probably sees Claude Fauriel, whom she last saw on her visit to Paris in 1828.

December

8 (Tues)   Richard Monckton-Milnes arrives in Paris, where he sees much of MWS. She reads his *'Poetry for the People', and Other Poems* (1840).

15   MWS attends the reinterment of Napoleon at Les Invalides. Milnes is also there, with William Makepeace Thackeray, who conceivably meets MWS. She is impressed by the contrasts between silence and martial music and by the realization that the coffin actually contains the remains of one whose name and influence filled the world (Letters, iii.19).

1841

January

7 (Thurs)   MWS returns to London. She finds accommodation at 84 Park Street.

In Journal entries for 11 and 12 this month and for 14 and 26 February she writes of her passionate desire, awakened by her visit to Italy, to leave England permanently. She has some hopes of at least visiting Egypt, Constantinople, or Sicily (Letters, iii.12–13).

23   Percy receives his B.A. from Cambridge.

CC reports to MWS Julia Robinson's comment that her family have 'sacrificed a brilliant society' for MWS's sake (Letters, iii.41). MWS will no longer associate with her.

February

14 (Sun) Sir Timothy, MWS learns or has recently learnt, is to give Percy £400 a year. Unlike previous payments, this is a gift, not repayable to the estate.

March

11 (Thurs) MWS orders from Moxon the latest editions of Lyell's *Principles of Geology* and Blackstone's *Commentaries on the Laws of England*. The Blackstone is presumably for Percy, who is thinking of studying law.

April

9 (Fri)   She visits the writer, art historian and feminist Anna Brownell Jameson. Fanny Kemble is probably there too (Letters, iii.15, n.1).

May

8 (Sat)   MWS and Percy holiday at Cowes on the Isle of Wight (until *c*.16–17). They tour the island and she feels cured of the 'wretched nervousness' she was suffering in London.

c. 17   They move to 34 Half Moon Street, London. She possibly visits Fanny Kemble soon afterwards (Letters, iii.15).

June

17 (Thurs) Mary Jane Godwin dies.

22   MWS and Percy set off for a summer holiday at or near Dolgelley in North Wales.

23   Moxon's trial on charges of blasphemous libel for publishing *Queen Mab* begins. He is prosecuted, but no sentence is imposed. In July he refuses MWS's offer of help with his expenses. Moxon sends her, and she is pleased with, Thomas Noon Talfourd's speech for the defence.

August

Late this month MWS and Percy return from Wales to 34 Half Moon Street.

December

6 (Mon) or 7 Mary Ellen Peacock probably visits. Seymour, pp. 460, 469, suggests that MWS hopes that Mary and Percy can be manoeuvred into falling in love. (She will marry and

soon be widowed in 1844. Her second marriage will be to George Meredith in 1849.)

7   Marriage of Aubrey Beauclerk and Rosa Robinson.

1842

MWS and Percy are paying half the Hunts' rent.

January
14 (Fri)   Recently MWS has read Sir George Grey's *Journals of Two Expeditions of Discovery in Northwest and Western Australia*, probably at least partly out of interest in her cousin Elizabeth Berry (daughter of Edward Wollstonecraft) who lives with her husband in New South Wales.

March
Late this month MWS and Percy go to Cowes again. They stay until about the beginning of June. In late April to early May Percy visits his half-sister, Ianthe, now married to Edward Jeffries Esdaile, in Somerset. Much of the time Percy's friend Alexander Knox also stays in Cowes.

At first MWS feels very unwell in Cowes. By 9 May she is much recovered, but still suffers bad headaches and cannot write or read easily, she tells CC (Letters, iii.25).

June
c. 1 (Wed)   MWS, Percy, and Knox come to stay at Exbury House, the home of Mr or 'Squire' Brett (first name not known) at Exbury in Hampshire, at the edge of the New Forest. By 5 they have returned to London, where MWS sees Gee Paul and Gregson (from whom she learns that she has less money than she hoped) and meets William Wordsworth at one of Rogers's breakfasts between 9 and 11.

12   MWS, Percy, Knox, and MWS's maid Marianne cross to Antwerp, en route for Germany and Italy, on the *Wilberforce*. MWS is keen for Knox to come, and will pay some of his expenses (Letters, iii.29); he is more socially adept than Percy (iii.32).

At Antwerp, where they stay on 13 and visit the cathedral, £16 is stolen from Percy's and Knox's room.

The group goes by train to Liège, where they stay at the Aigle Noire. On 14 they travel by carriage to Aachen and on 15 by rail to Cologne. From there a Rhine steamer takes them to Koblenz, where they stay the night at Hôtel Bellevue. They go on to Mainz and the Hôtel de Russie, Frankfurt (16). In Frankfurt she sees Marianna Hammond.

19 or 20   They arrive at Bad Kissingen and take lodgings. MWS drinks, and bathes in, the spa waters, goes for long walks, observes such visitors as the Queen of Württemberg and the King of Bavaria, and attempts without much success to learn German. This is made more difficult, she says, by her continuing headaches (Letters, iii.35).

July

19 (Wed)   They set off (by carriage) for Leipzig via the baths of Brükenau (19), Fulda, Buttlar (20), Eisenach – from which they visit the Wartburg – Gotha (21), Luther's monastery at Erfurt, and Weimar, where they tour the Goethe, Schiller, and Wieland sites. They arrive in Leipzig on 22 and go by rail to Berlin on 27. Here they stay at Hôtel Stadt Rom, Unter den Linden. On 28 MWS admires works by Correggio and Raphael and attends a production of Auber's opera *Masaniello*. The group visits the royal palace and the royal iron foundry on 29 and goes by rail to Dresden, where they have rooms on the third floor of the Palais Garni, on 30.

August

1 (Mon)   From Dresden they go to Rabenau in order to meet the composer Henry Hugh Pearson, who is to join the party. He has set songs by PBS and is working on an opera. Possibly at about this time he sets MWS's 'O listen while I sing to thee'.

15   In the gallery in Dresden she sees Alexis François Rio, whom she first met through Samuel Rogers. Rio's preference for intensity to technical perfection in Christian

art, as expressed in person in Dresden and Rome (see March 1843) and in his *Poésie Chrétienne* (1836), has some influence on MWS when she writes her *Rambles*; it affects particularly her attitude to Italian 'primitives' (*Novels and Selected Works*, 8.50–1).

16   MWS argues, in a letter to CC, that women are rarely happy living together; she claims that in breaking with (some of the) Robinsons last year she was bursting her fetters. (CC is planning to live with her friend Marianna Hammond.) In the same letter she says she finds Dresden beautiful but the Germans ugly, graceless and dirty.

17   She recommends Knox's poems to Hunt for their sensibility, facility, classical knowledge and originality. His *Giotto and Francesca, and Other Poems* is published later in the year. She also has great hopes for the tragedy he is writing, *The Heir of Cyprus*.

19   She is at a production of Weber's *Der Freischütz*.

27   They visit 'Saxon Switzerland', staying, after an adventurous walk, at the inn at the Grosse Winterberg. They reach Prague on 31, staying at the Drei Linden.

30   MWS's forty-fifth birthday.

September

2 (Fri) They stay at the Goldene Sonne, Budweis (Budejovice). They reach Linz on 4 and stay the night at the Goldene Löwe before moving on to Gmunden (5), Bad Ischl (6), Salzburg (7), Waldring (8), Schwaz (9), Innsbruck (10), the Brenner pass and Bressanone (11), Bolzano, Egna (12), Trento, and Riva (13). At Verona, on 14, they stay at Hôtel Gran Parigi. MWS goes with the others to see Juliet's alleged tomb and the Scaliger monuments. They proceed by way of Vicenza and Padua to Venice (16). The road along the banks of the Brenta powerfully reminds her of September 1818, when she went along it with the dying Clara: 'those who are enduring mental or corporeal agony are strangely alive to immediate external objects, and their imagination even exercises its wild power on them' (*Novels and Selected Works*, 8.269).

In Venice, after spending the night of 16 at the Leone Bianco, they move to the cheaper Hôtel d'Italia, not far from the Grand Canal and the Piazza. They see the usual sights, go to Luigi Ricci's opera *Chi dura vince* at the Fenice, and meet Milnes (who leaves for Constantinople on 30) and the radical John Temple Leader, whose manners MWS dislikes but whom she wants to cultivate with Percy's hoped-for political future in mind (Letters, iii.41).

October

1 (Wed)   MWS writes about the challenges of dealing with three young men including two generally pleasant but sometimes irritable invalids, Knox and Pearson; on 4 November, in low spirits herself, she says that Pearson has many 'unendurable' qualities (Letters, iii.44.)

19   The group leaves Venice and moves on, through Padua, Ferrara, and Bologna, to Florence (30). Here they stay at Casa Quadri, where the rent is a fairly expensive £4 per week. Their visits include the Pitti, the Uffizi, and Vallombrosa.

November

Early in the month MWS and Percy dine with Rev. John Sanford, his wife Elizabeth, and his daughter Anna Horatia.

4 (Fri)   An expected £100 has failed to arrive from MWS's banker. She fears that it has been stolen with the aid of a forged signature and feels, as often, that Fate is against her (Letters, iii.44). She feels worried and oppressed and sees Laura Galloni (Laurette Mason) and her sister Nerina Cini only rarely. (On 5 she confesses to CC that she does not get on with Laura as well as expected; later – see e.g. Letters, iii.55–6 – she is frustrated at the impossibility of helping Laura in the despondency and boredom of her married life in Florence.) By the end of the month she is seeing them a little more often.

On the evening of 4 MWS is at the opera with the Sanfords. She and Percy dine with them on 6.

5   The missing money arrives. By now she is sorry Pearson joined her party (Letters, iii.45). He tries to cause divisions between the others, is conceited and bad-tempered, and puts MWS to expense (Letters, iii.49–50). He leaves for Vienna, to the others' great relief, *c.* 11. But she regrets that Knox and Percy are not closer, and blames Pearson for this. She remains frustrated at Percy's shyness.

25   Someone has been spreading a rumour that MWS has
            married Knox. By this date she has heard about it from
            Gee Paul.

December
2 (Fri)   MWS and Percy (and probably Knox) see Laura Galloni
            and Nerina Cini.
3   The Sanfords call.
15   She is pleased, she writes to Hunt, at the opening up of
            China as a result of the Sino-British war of 1841–2; inter-
            vention in Afghanistan in 1839–42 was, by contrast, a
            mistake (Letters, iii.53 and n.10).
25   She writes to recommend Knox's *The Heir of Cyprus* to
            Macready, to whom it is about to be sent. It fails to
            achieve performance.

1843

MWS, Percy, and the anxious, ill, financially troubled and troubling
Knox (Letters, iii.57) remain in Florence this winter. They enjoy the
company of the Sanfords but find Lord Holland, secretary to the
embassy, rude. MWS sees but 'cuts' the Hoppners. The weather is
bad and she often feels ill or downcast.

February
23 (Thurs) or 25 Death of Everina Wollstonecraft, MWS's aunt.

March
By 20 (Mon) the group has reached Rome, where MWS and Percy stay
at Via Sistina 64. Knox takes separate accommodation.

In Rome MWS meets Rio again and visits galleries with him and his
wife. Percy does not share her taste for such activities. Rio leaves Rome
shortly before 7 May and his wife and children the following week.
21   Death of Robert Southey. MWS is anxious to obtain from
            his widow letters sent him by PBS in 1821 (Letters,
            iii.70), but apparently Southey destroyed them (iii.93).

April
4 (Tues)   Wordsworth succeeds Southey as Poet Laureate.
9–16   MWS and Mrs Rio go to the Holy Week 'ceremonies'
            (Letters, iii.69). She also sees Milnes, who has arrived

from Egypt, before his return to London at about the end of the month.

May

7 (Sun)   Moxon has suggested that she should write something for him – perhaps an essay or review, perhaps an account of her travels – and she, feeling better in Rome than in Florence, says that she may be able to produce something this summer, although she doubts it.

10   They leave Rome and set off for Sorrento, where they stay at the Cocumella, a former monastery. MWS likes it here except for the wind, the coastal reminders of Lerici, and her lack of funds. Knox, she feels, is still not a suitable companion for Percy, who longs for England.

June

1 (Thurs)   By this date they have visited Tasso's birthplace, the local caves, ruins and shore, the Piano di Sorrento, and Capodimonte. On 3 they visit Capri, where MWS notes the contrast between the beauty of 'this fairy island' and 'the hungry poverty of the hard-working peasants' (*Novels and Selected Works*, 8.373). On 22 or 23 they are at Pompeii, excavated further since she last saw it in December 1818; she has been reading Bulwer's *The Last Days of Pompeii* (1834), which 'has peopled its silence' (8.376).

July

c. 10 (Mon) They go to Amalfi, staying perhaps at the Albergo della Luna (*Novels and Selected Works*, 8.380, n.c). The following day they visit Ravello, Salerno, and Castellammare before returning to Sorrento. Here news reaches Knox of the death of his aunt, on whom he was financially dependent. MWS takes steps to have her furniture and pictures removed from the aunt's house. The group will go home earlier than intended.

13 or 15   They leave Sorrento. They sail from Naples to Marseille, arriving there on 19.

August

By early this month MWS has arrived in Paris, where she stays with CC at rue neuve de Clichy 3 until *c.* 25. Percy and Knox proceed to London by 13 (Sun).

In Paris MWS meets, through CC, a group of Italians in exile, supporters of Giuseppe Mazzini opposed to Austrian, papal and Bourbon rule of Italy. They include Ferdinando Gatteschi, Carlo Guitera, Carlo Romano, and Count Martini. MWS becomes passionately interested in their cause and welfare. She borrows 200 francs to give Gatteschi.

By 30 MWS arrives in London. Percy has found them 'gloomy and shocking' lodgings at 11 Portugal Street. She tells CC that the time abroad has done nothing to make him, for all his virtues, any more ambitious or desirous of good society (Letters, iii.83–4).

September
She sees Marianna Hammond.

11 (Mon) MWS and Percy move to White Cottage, Lower Richmond Road, Putney, on the Thames – Percy has bought a boat – and near Barnes Common.

Gatteschi is gathering material for an account of the Italian risings of 1831, on which MWS will draw in *Rambles*. At first she intends to raise money for him by arranging publication of his account, perhaps (Letters, iii.97) in *Blackwood's Edinburgh Magazine*.

20 She mentions, as quite often by now, that she is suffering from head pains. In the same letter, planning another visit to Paris, she explains to CC that, since she is by nature 'sadly and savagely independent', she must be completely independent during her stay (Letters, iii.90–1).

Moxon has again been asking MWS to write for him. She replies on 20 that she would 'prefer quieter work ... such as my lives for the Cyclopedia'. She feels she does this much better than 'romancing' (Letters, iii.93).

25 She asks Hunt to try to obtain work for her from John Forster at the *Foreign Quarterly*.

27 Partly in response to some new suggestion from Moxon she proposes an account – intended at this stage to be light and amusing – of her recent travels. Having looked over her notes she is already working fast. He approves of the idea. On about 29 she writes

again to ask if she should extend coverage to the 1840 tour, which will often complement that of 1842–3. Her letters written at the time will be one of her main sources, in addition to many published works including the Murray guides, Archibald Alison's *History of Europe*, Pietro Colletta's *Storia del Reame di Napoli dal 1734 sino al 1825*, Anna Jameson's *Sketches of Germany*, Luigi Lanzi's *Storia pittorica dell'Italia*, Vasari, and Sismondi. (See *Novels and Selected Works*, 8.50–1 and nn.)

October
Early this month Marianna Hammond stays with MWS for several days. Hunt visits.
By 8 (Sun) Moxon has advanced MWS £60 for the travel book. She says that she will return the money if fewer than 300 copies are sold.
16   Gee Paul visits.
By 28, after much delay, Gatteschi's manuscript has arrived.

Probably this autumn she reads, and finds baffling and boring, Eugène Sue's *Les Mystères de Paris*. She also reads Fredrika Bremer's *The President's Daughter*, translated by Mary Howitt.

November
MWS is working on *Rambles* in the mornings. She did not want to publish again (Letters, iii.105), but is driven by the desire to earn money to help Gatteschi (iii.101).
6 (Mon)   MWS meets and likes Enrico Mayer, the 'Italian educator and patriot' (Letters, iii.105, n.2).
10   Percy visits his grandfather at Field Place and then Aubrey and Rosa Beauclerk at St Leonards.

December
11 (Mon) About now MWS sets out for Paris, sailing from Folkestone. In Paris she again stays with CC and sees Gatteschi and other Italians, Anne Frances Hare, and probably the Boinville-Turners.

1844

January
18 (Thurs) Probable date when MWS leaves Paris. She reaches London *c*. 20–21. (See Letters, iii. 109–10, n.1.)

22   MWS breakfasts with Rogers, whom she continues to find unfailingly kind.

28   The first volume of MWS's *Rambles* is almost ready for the press and the second is well under way. In spite of eye problems she has managed some writing every day.

February
16 (Fri)   She has been reading Abraham Hayward's review of novels by Ida, Countess Hahn-Hahn in *The Edinburgh Review* for January; MWS dislikes it when 'lady novelists' create heroines so sentimental that they feel only for themselves (Letters, iii.113).

Late this month Martini and Guitera come to England and visit MWS. Martini is keen to sell a painting from Milan, allegedly by Titian, to the National Gallery. MWS, hopeful that some of the proceeds will go to Gatteschi, interests herself in the scheme, about which she wrote to Joseph Severn in December 1843. The painting is not, apparently, purchased. Seymour, pp. 493–4 and n.19, argues persuasively that it is a fake.

At about this time, or early next month, she sees Leader, to whom she is civil only for Percy's sake (see September 1842), the Hunts' son Henry, and Gee Paul.

March
c.10 (Sun)   She tells Moore that she finds his *History of Ireland* 'delightful'.

12   She may take Rogers to see Martini's picture (Letters, iii.117).

17   She writes to Rose Stewart, a new acquaintance of CC in Paris, for information on the history of Bohemia which she wants for *Rambles*.

28   She sees her goddaughter Rosalind 'Dina' Williams, married since 1842 to the Hunts' son Henry.

At the end of the month she reads *A New Spirit of the Age*, edited by Richard 'Hengist' Horne, which includes (vol. 2, pp. 224–32) an essay called in the contents list 'Mrs Shelley and Imaginative Romance'. High praise of *Frankenstein* as moral fable is followed by brief discussion of William Howitt's *Pantika* and Stephens' *Manuscripts of Erdely*, and of *Valperga*, which is 'below *Frankenstein* in genius' but still 'worthy of the author and of her high rank in the aristocracy of genius, as the daughter of Godwin and Mary Wollstonecraft, and the widow of Shelley'. She also reads Hunt's recently published *Poetical Works*.

April

Early in the month Percy visits Ianthe and Marianna Hammond visits MWS.

By 19 (Fri) MWS and Percy have somehow found more money to send Gatteschi.

20   With Sir Timothy at last on his deathbed, MWS warns Hunt that it will be difficult to pay him the £2000 he expects (see 30 Oct 1826). Nevertheless, he will go on receiving £30 a quarter. (See further *Letters*, iii.129–30, 138–9.)

24   Death of Sir Timothy Shelley (1753–1844). Percy succeeds to the baronetcy.

26   MWS sees Gregson in order to learn more about her and Sir Percy's new financial situation. This is far from ideal: Sir Timothy has left his personal fortune and portable property to his widow and children, a jointure of £500 must go on being paid to the widow and the £13 000 earlier disbursed to MWS and her son must be repaid; CC, Hunt, Ianthe and others become due for large legacies from PBS and some of his debts remain to be settled. Problems are exacerbated by Sir Timothy's having survived so much longer than expected, and by what MWS sees, probably not unfairly, as the grasping attitude of Lady Shelley and her daughters. (See further, on the financial situation, Seymour, pp. 498–9, and *Letters*, iii.131–2, 134, 157, 162–9 passim.) They need to borrow extensively, which is at least made easier by Percy's new title and prospects.

29   Percy goes to Sussex for the funeral of Sir Timothy.
Late this month or early next MWS sees Peacock.

May

Probably this month or next MWS entertains Lady Morgan and the novelist Catherine, Lady Stepney, and sees Marianna Hammond.
From 3 (Fri) or before, until 11 or after, MWS and Percy stay at Exbury.

June

c. 1 (Sat)-4   MWS and Percy stay at Field Place, which they find thoroughly dull (Letters, iii.135). She meets her mother-in-law, Elizabeth, Lady Shelley, for the first time and finds her and her family at least civil.

8   MWS tells Emily Godwin, widow of William Godwin, Jr, that she will provide her with £50 a year.

21   Abraham Hayward, the singer Adelaide Sartoris (Fanny Kemble's sister) and her husband Edward probably (Letters, iii.137) come to Putney to watch a Thames regatta with MWS.

27   Death of the publisher John Murray II.

July

3 (Wed)   The Sanfords dine with MWS; she visits them on 15 and probably (Letters, iii.145, n.1) on 23.
This month and in August Anne Frances Hare visits or stays with MWS.

August

1 (Thurs)   MWS publishes, as 'Mrs Shelley', *Rambles in Germany and Italy, in 1840, 1842, and 1843* (two volumes, Edward Moxon), dedicated to Samuel Rogers. Some advance copies were probably issued in late July (*Novels and Selected Works*, 8.51 and n.22). MWS tells Lady Morgan that the book 'has cost me more anxiety and pain than I can express' and Hunt that it is 'wretched', and feels that the 'the 2nd vol is best' (Letters, iii.145–6). Nevertheless many reviews are favourable, both to the work as travel account and to its political analyses. (*The Observer* for 11 is a notable exception: 'With her, as with all women, politics is a matter of the heart ... It is an idle and unprofitable theme for a woman.')

This month and probably into early next Gatteschi visits England, stays with Knox, and sees MWS.

3 and 10   A review of Caroline Halstead's *Richard the Third* in *The Athenaeum* nos 875–6 is possibly by MWS (Sunstein, p. 365; *Clairmont Correspondence*, pp. 404–5, n.2). If so, this is probably her last published work.

27   She tells an unknown correspondent that she is about to go to the country. If she does go, she is back by 5 September.

September
26 (Thurs)–1 October She stays at Sandgate with the Beauclerks.

October
14 (Mon)   She attends the wedding of Horatia Sanford and Hon. Frederick Methuen at St George's, Hanover Square. She may meet Rose Stewart later in the day (Letters, iii.157).

15–19   She is in Brighton.

27   She tells CC that although it would be useful if her son was more of a man of business, able to deal with the problems arising from his inheritance, his moderation, cheerfulness and equanimity make him 'the sheet anchor' of her life (Letters, iii.158).

November
*c.*15 (Fri)   MWS reads Hunt's *Imagination and Fancy; or Selections from the English Poets*. She writes to him, with a degree of enthusiasm she rarely expresses at this time in her life, about Dante's *Purgatorio* and *Paradiso*.

December
At some date between now and March 1846 (Letters, iii.162, n.1) the Scottish artist Joseph Noel Paton calls on MWS. His illustrations for PBS's *Prometheus Unbound* were published in the summer with a dedication to MWS.

6 (Fri)   As the extent of the burdens on the estate and other financial commitments becomes clearer, MWS feels that Percy is 'quite ruined' (Letters, iii.163).

By 7, Lady Shelley having moved out with everything she can take, Field Place has been let to Sir James Duke.

12	She sees Peacock (still involved as PBS's executor) and Gregson.
13	She goes to Horsham for a few days.
16	Hunt receives his £2000 legacy from PBS, with interest added.
23	MWS discusses, in a letter to CC, Harriet Martineau's letters to the *Athenaeum* on her cure by mesmerism; MWS is sceptical.

'The Swiss Peasant' and 'Ferdinando Eboli', by 'the Author of *Frankenstein*', are reprinted in Boston in *Friendship's Offering: a Christmas, New Year, and Birthday Present, for MDCCCXLV.*

1845

Publication of MWS's revised edition of PBS's *Essays, Letters from Abroad, Translations and Fragments.*

January
CC comes to stay with MWS. Some time during her visit MWS entertains her, Marianna Hammond, and Bartolomeo Cini, Nerina's husband.

11 (Sat)	MWS writes to Alexander Blackwood, of *Blackwood's Edinburgh Magazine*, to ask whether she should forward to him a story, sent to her from India, by Captain James Abbott.

April

1 (Tues)	After months of debate with MWS and others about her part in the financial settlement following the death of Sir Timothy, CC acknowledges receipt of her legacy of £6155 (including interest).
26	MWS entertains guests including Captain George Beauclerk.

May
In early May she dines with the writer Lucie, Lady Duff-Gordon, her husband Sir Alexander, and Lady Morgan.

c. 5 (Mon) CC returns to France.

MWS sees Lady Dorothea Campbell, visiting from Paris, several times. When she visits her on 23 Henrietta, Lady Dillon, widow of MWS's friend Lord Dillon, 'cuts' her.

June

By 6 (Fri) she has seen Jane Hogg, Marianna Hammond, and Gee Paul. She also sees Anne Frances Hare this summer.

26 Guests including Ada Ramsbottom and her sister Mrs Wilbraham, recently introduced to MWS by letter from CC, come to Putney for the regatta. Vincent Novello is also invited, but whether he comes is uncertain (*Letters*, iii.187–8). She enjoys the party, but feels in low spirits afterwards because expected income from rents on the estate has proved, after other expenses, non-existent, and it seems that future income is likely to decrease.

29 MWS and Henry Crabb Robinson breakfast with Rogers. Robinson finds her 'quiet and agreeable' (*On Books and Their Writers*, p. 654).

July

5 (Sat) She is reading Countess Hahn-Hahn's novel *Faustina*.

13 By this date she has probably read Kinglake's *Eothen* (see *Clairmont Correspondence*, p. 452).

16 She visits the Sanfords.

17 By this date she has invested in shares in the Hull and Selby railway.

21–*c.* 27 MWS and Percy stay at South Lodge, Horsham, home of the Beauclerks.

23 She writes to Milnes to ask him to persuade Sir Robert Peel to pay the £100 promised by his predecessor, Lord Melbourne, to David Booth, her friend Isabel's husband. Booth is now nearly eighty and prone to fits, delirium, and violence. She writes to Milnes again on the same subject in May 1846 ('Newly Uncovered Letters and Poems', pp. 70–1).

August

20 (Wed)-*c.* 28 MWS and Percy visit Elcott, near Hungerford, the new home of Lady Shelley and her daughters.

September
Probably this month (Letters, iii.204) she reads Thornton Hunt's *The Foster Brother*.

She suffers what her physician calls 'functional derangement in the nerves or brain' (Letters, iii.204), probably exacerbated by worry: on *c.* 10 (Wed) Gatteschi begins an attempt to blackmail MWS, threatening to make public – and no doubt invite misconstruction of – her affectionate and candid letters to him. Her head nevertheless feels better by 25. Knox, who is in Paris, takes up the responsibility of trying to extricate MWS from her predicament; in Paris he is able to discuss matters with CC. Gatteschi's letters to MWS are forwarded, unopened, to Knox. She also sends him £250, 'presumably the estimated cost of a complicated undercover operation' (Seymour, p. 506).

25   Percy is thinking of studying conveyancing.

c. 27–1 October She is at Broadstairs in Kent.

In letters to CC in September and October she frequently blames herself for being so easily duped by Gatteschi.

October
1 (Wed)   She sets off for Tunbridge Wells. On 4 she arrives in Brighton, where she sees much of Horace Smith and his family. On 13 she and Percy, who joined her *c.*10, are at the theatre with Smith's daughters, with one of whom, Laura, MWS briefly thinks Percy is likely to fall in love. PBS's brother John and his wife are also at the theatre but ignore her, MWS says (Letters, iii.234); they call on her, however, on 15 and she is struck by John's resemblance to PBS.

11   Thanks to Knox's efforts French officers, sent by the prefect of police Gabriel Delessert, seize Gatteschi's papers. Knox is allowed to remove MWS's letters, which are subsequently destroyed. On 16 she hears from him that the French police have agreed to let it be understood that the motive for the seizure was – as is already widely supposed – political; Gatteschi himself is unlikely to realize her involvement.

16   MWS and Percy return to Putney.

22   She tells Louisa Kenney that through illness she must postpone writing her father's life. (For the date see *Letters*, iii.241, n.1.)

26   Knox returns from Paris. He stays for some time with or near MWS and Percy.

28   Major George Byron, who claims to be Lord Byron's son, has told the bookseller Thomas Hookham that he possesses letters written by PBS and MWS. Some of the letters are genuine, but many are forged. MWS is desperate, so soon after the Gatteschi affair, to avoid scandal and so agrees to pay the Major for batches of letters.

November

1 (Sat)   MWS has sent a note to Charles Clairmont through CC. They have been out of contact for sixteen years because of his embarrassment at having persuaded her to lend him money in 1829 and his belief that she was offended with him. He now explains this and re-establishes cordial relations.

11   Percy begins study with a conveyancer in London. It is not known how long he perseveres with this.

12   Major Byron acknowledges receipt of £30 from MWS.

16   Death of MWS's friend Lady Canterbury.

19   MWS dates her poem 'The Death of Love' ('Newly Uncovered Letters', pp. 72–3).

22   Percy and MWS have sold Castle Goring, a Shelley property, to Captain George Pechell for £11250. This will enable them to pay off more debts and to buy a house.

Some time after 22 MWS goes with Gee Paul to visit Gee's father at St Leonard's Lodge, Horsham. She is back in Putney by 1 December.

December

1 (Mon)   MWS and Percy have arranged to buy a house at 24 Chester Square, London.

Early this month she sees Jane Hogg and Elizabeth Sanford.

11   Percy goes to Sussex to see the Duke of Norfolk about his intention of standing as MP for Horsham. MWS deprecates the Duke's notorious recent declaration that a

pinch of curry powder in hot water will warm the stomachs of the poor. She supports repeal of the Corn Laws, although she realizes the political complexity of the situation (Letters, iii.269–70) and admits that she particularly hopes that repeal will come before the next election because the Corn Laws are 'a difficult bit' for a candidate – in other words for Percy (Letters, iii.265).

11   She sends CC £100 to sort out Knox's affairs in Paris: he needs to dispose of an expensive apartment. MWS feels that she is robbing Percy, but Knox, although now writing articles for the *Morning Chronicle*, as yet has insufficient funds to pay for himself.

25   Death of Charles George Beauclerk, father of MWS's friends Aubrey and George Beauclerk and Gee Paul.

This month or next MWS reads Martineau's *Forest and Game-law Tales*. 'The Dream', by 'the Author of Frankenstein' is reprinted in Philadelphia in *Leaflets of Memory: an Annual for MDCCCXLVI*.

1846

January
She dines with the Sanfords on 2 (Fri) and goes to see Gee Paul on 3. Probably this month she reads Hunt's *Stories from the Italian Poets*.

22   She sees Hookham.

30 or 31 She is angered by Bulwer's dismissal of PBS's poetry – he questions whether 'any general idea is to be found buried amid the gaudy verbiage' – in his translation of *The Poems and Ballads of Schiller* (1844). Bulwer has, MWS tells Moxon, mistaken the spirit of the times.

February
27 (Fri) or 28 She goes to see Peacock, who tells her that she should not have given Major Byron money. For the present, however, as her letters to Hookham over the next few days make clear, she remains ready to offer more. Only in September does she begin to refuse further payment. (See Letters, iii.297–8.)

March

Early this month MWS moves to 24 Chester Square. At some point between her move and summer 1847 she breakfasts with the German novelist Ida, Countess Hahn-Hahn.

12 (Thurs) MWS is taken seriously ill. Dr Gideon Mantell, who is a near neighbour, and Dr John Ayrton Paris, President of the Royal College of Physicians, are summoned. They diagnose 'neuralgia of the heart'.

Some time after this month MWS translates from Italian two chapters of Laura Galloni's novel *Inez de Medine* (Naples, 1846), for which she has asked her to find an English publisher. (See *Maurice*, ed. Tomalin, p. 150.)

April

Probably early this month MWS and Percy go to Cowes. Her doctors have recommended the seaside. They return to Chester Square in mid-May. The holiday does her, she feels, no good (Letters, iii.287).

May

*c.*15 (Fri) MWS is displeased to learn that Medwin is writing a biography of PBS. She feels that in her editions she 'vindicated the memory of my Shelley and spoke of him as he was – an angel among his fellow mortals – lifted far above this world ... and his works are an immortal testament giving his name to posterity in a way more worthy of him than my feeble pen is capable of doing'. She must 'deprecate the publication of particulars and circumstances injurious to the living', particularly 'in these publishing, inquisitive, scandal-mongering days' (Letters, iii.284). She is concerned at the possible effect not only on herself but on CC and Ianthe. Perhaps on 23 (Letters, iii.286, n.1), Medwin sends a letter in which he says that he can only desist from publishing the work if she indemnifes him for the considerable financial loss involved, including the £250 he claims to have been paid by a publisher. She is outraged at this blackmail and does not answer the letter.

June

22 (Mon) Mantell dines with MWS and Percy.

July

c. 18 (Sat)   She sets off for Baden-Baden, arriving *c.* 25. She stays at 153 Promenade. She enjoys the company of Anne Frances Hare, her children, and her sister Eleanor Paul. She also sees the Sanfords. After the first week she suffers an attack involving pain in the spine. For some time after a long walk on 25 or 26 August she can hardly move.

August

21 (Fri)   Death of MWS's mother-in-law, Elizabeth, Lady Shelley.

25   By now MWS is anxious for Percy to join her in Baden; the mere thought of Chester Square, where CC is staying with him, makes her feel ill (Letters, iii.292–3). He joins her at some point in September.

Hunt has been asking for yet more money, and MWS feels less sympathetic than before (Letters, iii.295).

October

Late this month she returns from Baden. Her health has only slightly improved.

31 (Sun)   Mantell calls.

November

Early this month she sees Charles Robinson, brother of Julia, Rosa, and Eliza, who has just arrived from New Zealand.

Some time before 12 (Thurs) she reads Hunt's *Wit and Humour*, which he has sent her.

24   She writes to Octavian Blewitt, secretary of the Royal Literary Fund, to appeal for a renewal of financial assistance to David Booth. She writes with further details on 4 and 6 December.

December

Early this month MWS and Percy are at Elcott House, the home of his late grandmother.

5 (Sat)   Death of David Booth. The Royal Literary Fund grants Isabel Baxter Booth £50.

21   Mantell comes to dinner.

'The Sisters of Albano', by 'the Author of *Frankenstein*', is reprinted in Boston in *Friendship's Offering: a Christmas, New Year, and Birthday*

Present, for MDCCCXLVII. 'Euphrasia: a Tale of Greece', by 'Mrs Shelley', is reprinted in Philadelphia in *Leaflets of Memory: an Illuminated Annual for MCCCXLVII.*

1847

January

Early this month Mantell gives MWS a copy of his *Thoughts on Animalcules, or A Glimpse of the Invisible World Revealed by the Microscope* (1846).

26 (Wed) Marianne Hunt writes to ask for more money and complains that when she called MWS would not see her or even send a message to the door. MWS's reply explains that she and her son have yet to repay the loan of £200 they took out last year for the Hunts' benefit and must pay a £3800 bond of PBS's and £1000 for repairs on the estate. She asks forgiveness for not seeing Marianne, but she 'could not see her' (Letters, iii.306).

February

1 (Tues) She orders Moxon's cheap editions of Richard Henry Dana's *Two Years Before the Mast* and a work by Thomas Pringle, probably *African Sketches.*

March

19 (Fri) She writes to reassure CC that she would willingly encourage a marriage between her and the lawyer and author Walter Coulson, whom they have known for many years; she has no intention of taking him for herself, or of marrying anyone, and is indeed 'married to Percy' (Letters, iii.307). She is ill again, confined to bed by the orders of the Dr Smith who is now attending her.

29 Charles Robinson visits.

29 MWS expresses the not uncommon contemporary view that too much money is being spent on combating the Irish famine.

April

She possibly entertains a group including CC, Coulson, Knox, and Peacock (Letters, iii.311 and n.1).

May

27 (Thurs)   She has read Hayward's *Verses of Other Days*. She invites him to call on 31, when she also expects PBS's sisters.

June

10 (Thurs)   Hunt has sent her his latest book, *Men, Women, and Books: a Selection of Sketches, Essays, and Critical Memoirs*. On 22 he is awarded a pension of £200 a year.

16   Nerina's brother-in-law Tommaso Cini visits. About now MWS also sees Dina Williams Hunt.

17 or 18   MWS is deemed well enough to go to Brighton, where she stays at 13 Bedford Square. At first – and sometimes later in her visit – she finds the town too noisy, but soon begins to feel rather better. Percy is away on various yachting expeditions; later in the summer he goes to Germany, Denmark and Norway. Knox visits MWS on 20.

July

11 (Sun)   Medwin's *Life* is about to be published. MWS asks Hunt to use his influence to persuade the newspapers to ignore it. He feels that this risks drawing too much attention to the work, and in the event its revelations are not as scandalous as MWS feared. Nevertheless she does not read it.

13   Gee Paul comes to Brighton. MWS also spends time with Gee's sister, Diana, Lady Vane.

August

On or before 1 (Sun) Isabel Baxter Booth comes to Brighton to see MWS, leaving probably by 9. CC stays between about 9 and 23 and Percy has arrived by 21.

30   MWS's fiftieth birthday. She and Percy return to London briefly. They see Hunt. She is in considerable pain.

September

1 (Wed)   MWS and Percy go to stay with his aunts at Elcott House for a few days. She buys for £30 an open carriage which belonged to Lady Shelley.

4   She asks CC to try to obtain for her French accounts of the duc de Praslin's recent murder of his wife and suicide.

Some time this autumn Percy and MWS visit Monmouthshire.

November
'The Parvenue', by 'Mrs Shelley', is reprinted in Boston in *The Amaranth; or, Token of Remembrance: a Christmas and New Year's Gift for MDCCCXLVIII.*
She sees Trelawny and tells him that Percy has fallen in love with an unsuitable young woman. This does not, it seems, last long. Probably about now MWS meets a young widow, Jane St John (1820–99). She is particularly interested in, and gets on very well with, MWS, but also soon meets Percy.

December
This month George Gilfillan's article 'Female Authors. – No. III. – Mrs Shelley' is published in *Tait's Edinburgh Magazine*, pp. 850–4. It is reproduced in the New York *Eclectic Magazine of Foreign Literature* in February 1848 and in *Littell's Living Age* in March 1848.
25 (Sat)   Gee Paul dies. She 'shed a charm over' MWS's life by her affectionate interest (Letters, iii.331).

1848

March
18 (Sat)   MWS probably sees CC. On *c.* 20 Jane St John comes to stay, leaving *c.* 10 April. MWS finds her sweet and gentle (Letters, iii.334, 339). By 10 June – presumably some months earlier – Percy has asked her to marry him.
28   MWS, writing to her cousin's widower Alexander Berry in Australia, talks of her dislike of the recent French revolution. While the revolutionaries in Italy and Germany seek political change, the French seek social change, spreading their 'wicked and desolating principles'. In England the Chartists are to be guarded against (Letters, iii.335–6).

Percy is canvassing as a radical candidate for Horsham. By April, however, he has withdrawn from active politics.

April
MWS probably sees CC after 8 (Sat).
10   The intended Chartist march to the Houses of Parliament, much feared by MWS and others, is prevented.

June

22 (Thurs)   Sir Percy Florence Shelley marries Jane St John at St George's, Hanover Square, London. MWS and Anne Frances Hare are among those present. The new Lady Shelley brings with her a fortune of £15 000.

July

While the newly-weds are on honeymoon in the Lake District MWS, in poor health, goes to Sandgate, returning to London on 29 (Sat). Knox is with her for some time.

August

c. 1 (Tues)   MWS and her son and daughter-in-law move into Field Place. Knox visits on 13.

October

By 19 (Thurs) she is in Brighton, staying initially at the Pier Hotel. Percy, Jane, and Knox are with her some of the time.

25   She writes to support the music critic Edward Holmes's application for a grant from the Royal Literary Fund.

November

17 (Fri)   Marianne Hunt has written again to ask for an addition to the annuity the Shelleys already pay. MWS tells her she cannot help: Percy's election costs from the spring must be met and the estate involves many expenses.

22   She has a bad attack. CC comes to see her on 23.

27   She leaves Brighton and goes, with Percy and Jane, to 77 Warwick Square, London, an apartment they have recently taken.

December

MWS is worried because Jane Shelley is ill and Knox has been jilted by a woman whom he seemed certain to marry.

1849

January

By 28 (Sun) the three Shelleys are back at Field Place, where Knox is a regular visitor.

February

5 (Mon)   Gee Paul's son Aubrey is visiting for a few days. John Hastings Touchet, a friend of Percy, comes *c.* 20–25. On 23 Percy and Jane go to London to consult Jane's doctor, who thinks she is gravely ill but may well recover. MWS, very worried, visits them briefly in the first week of March.

March

c. 14 (Wed)   Jane Hogg and her daughter Dina Hunt are visiting MWS at Field Place.

Soon after 19 she goes to London again until about the end of the month. While there she sees Jane Hogg.

April

Within a few days of 7 (Sat) Percy and Jane have returned to Field Place. Hellen and Margaret Shelley, PBS's sisters, stay briefly.

Probably this month, MWS writes to Laura Galloni offering to undertake further work on her novels. She refuses (*Letters*, iii.365, n.4), perhaps in deference to MWS's state of health.

May

Early in the month Clara Clairmont, daughter of Charles Clairmont and niece of CC, comes to stay at Field Place, where she meets Alexander Knox. Encouraged particularly by Lady Shelley, they soon decide to marry.

June

16 (Sat)   Marriage of Knox and Clara Clairmont at St George's, Hanover Square. They have not informed CC of their plans. She appears at first not to disapprove, but is soon sending furious letters condemning the match to her brother Charles, the bride's father, who for a time does not know what to make of the very different information he receives from CC, Knox, Clara, and his son Wilhelm Clairmont, who is with CC. She blames MWS for the hasty marriage, claims to Charles that Knox was MWS's lover, and breaks off all communication with her. (See *Clairmont Correspondence*, p. 503 f.) At the root of her anger, no doubt, is the old tension between the stepsisters; Lady Shelley later claims that – probably

during a visit by CC in May – MWS, with unexpected passion, begged her daughter-in-law 'Don't go, dear! don't leave me alone with her! She has been the bane of my life ever since I was three years old!' (Florence Marshall, *The Life and Letters of Mary Wollstonecraft Shelley*, 1889, 2.312). At MWS's death in February 1851 CC writes to Percy and fills most of her letter with complaints about not being told MWS was ill, the way she (CC) has been treated by Percy and Jane, and the general unhappiness of her lot (*Clairmont Correspondence*, pp. 536–7). Her anger continues for some years.

September
14 (Fri)   Jane and Percy Shelley set off for Paris. Jane is on the whole better but has been told to winter in a warmer climate by her doctor. She is, MWS tells Peacock, 'a woman such as poets love to paint' (Letters, iii.372).

c. 27–28   MWS sets off to join the others in Paris. She may see Peacock in London before she leaves.

Some time this autumn the Shelleys proceed to Nice, staying at Maison Serrat. MWS is sometimes well enough to ride a donkey into the hills.

December
26 (Wed)   William and Robert Brough's *Frankenstein; or the Model Man* opens at the Adelphi Theatre for 54 performances.

1850

February
2 (Sat)   Death of Charles Clairmont, brother of CC and step-brother of MWS.

April
23 (Tues)   Death of William Wordsworth.
Probably late this month the Shelleys move on from Nice to northern Italy.

May
c. 19 (Sun) They arrive at Cadenabbia. Soon after 26 they set off
for England.

June
17 (Mon)   They arrive at Field Place.

July
At some point this month they stay at Elcott.
MWS visits the Knoxes.

August
Anne Frances Hare comes to Field Place with her daughter.

September
Visitors include Aubrey Paul, Gee's son, and possibly Eliza, Rosalind,
and Laura Smith.
In the autumn MWS, Percy and Jane go to Chester Square to avoid
the dampness of Field Place.

November
15 (Fri)   MWS writes to Octavian Blewitt of the Royal Literary
Fund to ask whether Isabella Baxter Booth can be given a
further grant. He replies on 18 that by the rules of the
fund she cannot receive more. Instead, Percy agrees to
provide her with £50 a year.

Probably in November or December Peacock dines at 24 Chester
Square. He is possibly accompanied by his daughter Ellen and her
new husband George Meredith.
MWS's 'The Brother: a Tale of Greece', a reprint of 'Euphrasia: a
Tale of Greece', appears in the New York *Keepsake: a Gift for the
Holidays*.

1851

January
Isabel Baxter Booth offers to come and help nurse MWS, who is
increasingly weak. On 23 (Thurs) she goes into a coma.

February

1 (Sat)   Death of MWS at 24 Chester Square. According to the death certificate she died of 'Disease of the Brain Supposed Tumour in left hemisphere, of long standing'. Modern analysis of the symptoms she recorded suggests 'that she may have died of meningioma, a tumour in the covering of the brain that can spread into the brain itself' (Betty T. Bennett, Letters, iii.389).

8   She is buried at St Peter's church in Bournemouth, near the Shelleys' new home at Boscombe. Since she expressed a desire to be buried with her parents in St Pancras churchyard, their remains are transferred, by 7 March, to the same grave in Bournemouth. Some time between then and 1889 the ashes of PBS's heart are also buried there (see Seymour, Appendix 1), as is Sir Percy Florence Shelley in 1889 and Lady Shelley in 1899.

Sources

Works by MWS

The Journals of Mary Shelley 1814–1844, ed. Paula R. Feldman and Diana Scott-Kilvert, 2 vols, Oxford, 1987.

The Letters of Mary Wollstonecraft Shelley, ed. Betty T. Bennett, 3 vols, Baltimore and London, 1980–8. These volumes are supplemented by Bennett's 'Newly Uncovered Letters and Poems by Mary Wollstonecraft Shelley', *Keats-Shelley Journal*, vol. 46, 1997, pp. 51–74.

Frankenstein or the Modern Prometheus: the 1818 Text, ed. Marilyn Butler, Oxford, 1993.

Maurice; or The Fisher's Cot, ed. Claire Tomalin, London, 1998.

Mary Shelley: Collected Tales and Stories, ed. Charles E. Robinson, Baltimore and London, 1976.

Mary Shelley, *Novels and Selected Works*, ed. Nora Crook, 8 vols, London, 1996.

The 'Frankenstein Notebooks': a Facsimile Edition of Mary Shelley's Manuscript Novel, 1816–17, ed. Charles E. Robinson, 2 vols, New York and London, 1996.

Valperga: or, the Life and Adventures of Castruccio, Prince of Lucca, ed. Stuart Curran, Oxford, 1997.

Letters and journals of Godwin, CC and PBS

William Godwin, Journal, Abinger Papers, Dep. e.196–227, Bodleian Library, Oxford.

The Letters of Percy Bysshe Shelley, ed. Frederick L. Jones, 2 vols, Oxford, 1964.

The Journals of Claire Clairmont, ed. Marion Kingston Stocking, Cambridge, Mass., 1968.

The Clairmont Correspondence: Letters of Claire Clairmont, Charles Clairmont, and Fanny Imlay Godwin, ed. Marion Kingston Stocking, Baltimore and London, 2 vols, 1995.

Shelley and his Circle, 1773–1822, ed. Kenneth Neill Cameron and Donald H. Reiman, Cambridge, Mass., 8 vols, 1961–86. [Manuscripts, mainly letters, of Wollstonecraft, Godwin, the Shelleys and other connections.]

Other

Jane Blumberg, *Mary Shelley's Early Novels: 'This Child of Imagination and Misery'*, London, 1993.

J. L. Bradley, *A [P.B.] Shelley Chronology*, Basingstoke and London, 1993.

The Correspondence of Aaron Burr and his Daughter, Theodosia, ed. Mark van Doren, New York, 1929.

Benjamin Colbert, 'Contemporary Notice of the Shelleys' *A Six Weeks' Tour*: Two New Early Reviews', *Keats-Shelley Journal*, vol. 48, 1999, pp. 22–8.

Jane Dunn, *Moon in Eclipse: a Life of Mary Shelley*, London, 1978.

Paula R. Feldman, 'Mary Shelley and the Genesis of Moore's Life of Byron', *Studies in English Literature 1500–1900*, vol. 20, 1980, pp. 611–20.

Steven Earl Forry, *Hideous Progenies: Dramatizations of 'Frankenstein' from Mary Shelley to the Present*, Philadelphia, 1990.

Richard Holmes, *Shelley: the Pursuit*, London, 1974.

Nicholas A. Joukovsky, 'Mary Shelley's Last Letter?' *Notes & Queries*, vol. 242, 1997, p. 338.

W. H. Lyles, *Mary Shelley: an Annotated Bibliography*, New York, 1975.

Florence Marshall, *The Life and Letters of Mary Wollstonecraft Shelley*, 2 vols, London, 1889.

Peter H. Marshall, *William Godwin*, New Haven and London, 1984.

The Journal of Thomas Moore, ed. Wilfred S. Dowden with Barbara G. Bartholomew and Joy L. Linsley, 6 vols, Newark, London and Toronto, 1983–91.

The Letters of Thomas Moore, ed. Wilfred S. Dowden, 2 vols, Oxford, 1964.

The Diary of Dr John William Polidori, 1816, Relating to Byron, Shelley, etc., ed. W. M. Rossetti, London, 1911.

Charles E. Robinson, 'Editing and Contextualizing the *Frankenstein Notebooks*', *Keats-Shelley Journal*, vol. 46, 1997, pp. 36–44.

Henry Crabb Robinson, *On Books and their Writers*, ed. Edith J. Morley, 3 vols, London, 1938.

Maud Rolleston, *Talks with Lady Shelley*, 1897.

William St Clair, *The Godwins and the Shelleys: the Biography of a Family*, London and Boston, 1989.

Miranda Seymour, *Mary Shelley*, London, 2000.

Emily W. Sunstein, *Mary Shelley: Romance and Reality*, Baltimore, 1989.

Emily W. Sunstein, 'Young Mary Godwin', *Keats-Shelley Journal*, vol. 45, May 1996.

Index